R. W. Thompson.

Applerigg

Kendal.

ALBERT SCHWEITZER
AN INTRODUCTION

DR SCHWEITZER IN HIS STUDY
ON THE VILLAGE STREET, GÜNSBACH

ALBERT SCHWEITZER

AN INTRODUCTION

BY

JACQUES FESCHOTTE

With two addresses by
Albert Schweitzer

LONDON
ADAM AND CHARLES BLACK
1955

FIRST PUBLISHED 1954
REPRINTED 1955

A. AND C. BLACK LIMITED
4, 5 AND 6 SOHO SQUARE, LONDON, W.I

TRANSLATED FROM THE FRENCH
BY JOHN RUSSELL

MADE IN GREAT BRITAIN
PRINTED BY W. & J. MACKAY & CO., LTD.,
CHATHAM

NOTE

The absence of any brief but adequate account of the life and work of Albert Schweitzer justifies the publication in English of this new study by an intimate friend who has had particular opportunities to know his subject in his Alsatian village home.

A permanent value is given to M. Feschotte's book by its inclusion, at Schweitzer's suggestion, of two of his most recent writings: an account of an episode in his childhood, and his important address on the problem of ethics in the evolution of human thought, delivered on his installation as a member of the French Academy in 1952.

CONTENTS

ALBERT SCHWEITZER AT GÜNSBACH

The last chord of César Franck's Third Chorale was still echoing round the church when Dr Schweitzer closed the lid of the organ and put out the lamp. We felt our way down the creaking wooden staircase. The door opened on to the Munster valley. Shadows were already dark on the surrounding foothills of the Vosges. Lights shone out peacefully from village windows. The road rang with the sound of our footsteps; there was little traffic at nightfall. From time to time we passed a belated workman, or a man from the vineyards; and with each of these the Doctor exchanged the traditional "Good night!" Walking on past his house, we soon reached the turn in the road, where the view extends to the far end of the valley in the direction of the Schlucht Pass; peaceable Munster lay hidden there. The little railway-line which runs from Munster to Colmar had lapsed into silence. A murmur of running water from the Fecht grew louder in the perfumed air.

The Doctor was silent for a long time, as he usually is after playing the organ. But when we came to the simple bench on which he loves to sit, we stopped. When he began to speak, it was as if he were continuing aloud some train of thought that had hitherto been carried on in silence within him. The accent of his native province seemed, as always, to heighten the grave and sonorous quality of his utterance.

9

"It'll be quiet at Lambaréné too," he said. "There'll be a sleepy feeling in all the huts, except where there are people who cry out in pain. All the animals are asleep. Doctors and nurses are hoping to get some rest. Yes, it's exactly the same moment in the day . . ." Another silence: the Doctor's thoughts are with his hospital. He is making his last round before going to his room; he goes to every ward, and misses nothing. "Good night, my children." He once told me that if he did not do this, they would never go to sleep. And we know that he too could not rest if he had not seen that all was in order.

And so it had been, every evening, for five consecutive years: the longest of his sojourns in Lambaréné. We had begun to wonder anxiously if he would ever come back, and if we should be able to visit him at Günsbach and walk once more, by his side, in the cool of twilight.

That whole day had been like a miracle for me. Time had been abolished. When the bus from Colmar stopped at the Günsbach crossroads, the Doctor's lofty silhouette was outlined, as before, on the white road. I could hardly speak: my heart was beating too fast. He took me into his arms, and at once I recognised him. He was thinner, certainly; and more lined, and whiter; but his eyes shone more brightly than ever, and beneath the trailing moustaches the mouth was eloquent of loving goodwill. I followed him happily into the house where, for month after month and year after year, the faithful Madame Martin had been waiting for him to come back. At first we spoke of those who were dear to us—our families, our friends, and those whom we should never see again. Madame Schweitzer was away in the Black Forest, resting. I was given my old white room with its wide view across the valley and the Vosges. Before lunch, we sat in the big communal "office", where the Doctor has his desk, and Madame Martin hers—one that overflows with letters and books whenever the postman calls. There were native sculptures—animals in wood and ivory that astonished in spite of their crudity—and with them other souvenirs of every sort: a watch given to Schweitzer by the great organist Guilmant, and now lovingly framed; drawings and paintings of African and Alsatian scenes; family photographs. It seemed as if the Doctor had never left us—as if we had parted the day before, and the war, the Occupation, the whole enormous drama of which none can see the end, were nothing but a bad dream. Such, at least, was the effect of the conviction, the sense of certainty, that radiated from the Doctor.

Friendship, for him, has the strength of religion; and he began to talk of many subjects, as he alone can talk: Strasbourg, music, our old friends in Paris, the moral drama of our times, the lesson of Goethe, the results of a new remedy for leprosy. Schweitzer has enough knowledge, and enough moral strength, for a dozen "exceptional men"; and he moves as easily among the practical arrangements of everyday life as among the eternal problems of religion and philosophy. After lunch, he went to his room to write. But before long the usual flood of visitors, friends old and new, came pouring into the house. It's always like that when the news gets out that he's at home. How numberless they are—the people whose hearts and minds have known the blessing of his company! And yet Madame Martin was waiting, with the more urgent and important of his letters: that post-bag in which the humblest requests lie side by side with letters from reigning sovereigns, and unknown admirers crowd in among the most famous of living men. Dinner was as cordial as lunch, and afterwards we went along to the church. The lovely light of the end of the day seemed to saturate the forests of the Vosges and the valley pastures. "It won't bore you to hear the organ for a little while?" asked the Doctor with a smile. And the spirit of Bach, resurrected in Schweitzer, poured forth its healing power.

As we paused on the way home, night fell and the first stars shone out above the shadowed mountains. The scattered lamps of the village were like humble reflections of these greater beacons. The conversation began again. Schweitzer returned to Goethe. He, better than anyone, has understood not merely the intellectual significance of Goethe, which is now greater and more topical than ever, but also his continual curiosity, his passion for knowledge. He described how Goethe would leave his grand house at Weimar and wander across the fields, talking to the peasants, learning how to tend and graft his fruit-trees according to the latest methods, and meditating, at the same time, the sublime thoughts which later became Part II of *Faust*. Schweitzer, too, is by turns homely and sublime; and his thoughts swung back to Alsace, where he was born, and where once again his footsteps rang out on the road that led back to the sleeping village of Günsbach. He told me that on the voyage from Africa his ship had passed another, fully laden with the bodies of soldiers killed in the war. This reminded him of how other soldiers, killed on Alsatian soil during the war of 1914–18, had been dug up after the Armistice and taken home. What was the point, he wondered, of disturbing these poor remnants?

"If I am called to God during one of my visits here,"
he said firmly to me, "I want to rejoin my own people
in the little cemetery here. But if I fall into my last
sleep in Africa—why then, I should want to be buried
in Lambaréné. It's only logical to lie where one falls,
and the earth is God's earth, no matter where it is."

We fell silent again. It was striking ten when we
saw the Doctor's house loom up in the shadows. All
thoughts of death were cast aside when he went, as he
has gone for half a century, to work in the silence and
solitude of the night. He was nearing the end of that
moral treatise for which so many of us, in so many parts
of the world, are waiting in happy impatience. He was
already far from us, in his thoughts. I stayed for a
moment outside on the road. The Doctor reached his
room, which stands on the ground floor, only a little
above street-level. He sat at his table; through the
wide-open window with its creeper-covered frame I
could see part of the room. It was as simple as a monk's
cell. On the white door were two dark shadows: his
jacket, and his big black hat. He was writing; his forehead, with the greying locks thrust back, hung over the
table. The lamplight reached just as far as the road, but
I knew that the invisible radiance of his spirit was
lighting at that very moment the lives of innumerable
friends of Schweitzer, known and unknown; and that
this illumination was as vital to them as the healing care
which he has lavished on the sufferers of Lambaréné.

Part I

HIS LIFE

I. FAMILY, CHILDHOOD AND ADOLESCENCE.

At the beginning of his *Memoirs of Childhood and Youth*, Albert Schweitzer has established, with his usual sobriety, and with the completest precision, the place and the circumstances of his birth. All those who have written about him have made use of this passage. But often they have subjected it to pointless transformations; and so I particularly want to quote it verbatim:

"I was born on January 14th 1875 at Kaysersberg, Haute-Alsace, in the little house with a turret that you can see at the top of the town, to the left as you go out of it. In this little area, most of the inhabitants are Catholics; my father was the pastor and preceptor of the evangelical community . . . The name of Kaysersberg derives from the great preacher Geiler de Kaysersberg (1445–1510) . . . The year 1875 was famous for its wines. When I was a boy I was proud to have been born in a good vintage year, and in the same town as Geiler de Kaysersberg."

The general appearance of Kaysersberg has not changed a great deal since that period. The birthplace of Albert Schweitzer is intact, though the last war dealt heavy blows to this picturesque town among the vineyards of the Upper Rhine. But the beautiful church with its old organ, so dear to the Doctor's heart, and its big reredos was spared, and so was the neighbouring Hôtel de Ville, whose ancient *boiseries* have survived many a war and many an occupation. In point of fact, however, this scene, dominated by the high tower of the ruined Château, did not become familiar to Schweitzer until much later. For he was barely six months old when his father was nominated pastor of Günsbach, an agreeable village some fifteen miles from Kaysersberg, in the valley of Munster, and at the very feet of the Vosges. Schweitzer's mother was quite at home in her new environment, for she was the daughter of a very remarkable man, Pastor Schillinger, who was himself from Muhlbach, a village a little higher up on the other side of the valley.

Albert Schweitzer has described what his parents remembered of his earliest years: how he was fragile, and even weakly, when he came into the world. For several months it was even uncertain that he would live. But, little by little, a sturdy little boy grew up in place of the delicate baby. And he grew up as one of a happy family, with his brother and three sisters (a sixth child, a little girl, died prematurely).

"My earliest recollection," he tells us, "is of the Devil." But there is a streak of Alsatian humour in this surprising remark: for he explains that when he was still quite small, from the age of three onwards, his parents took him to church on Sundays. He enjoyed this enormously. But he was immensely intrigued—if not terrified—by the apparition of a bearded head above the organ: whenever the pastor was praying, and when he mounted the pulpit, this head disappeared. "It can only be the Devil himself!" young Albert concluded . . . until one day he realised that it was merely the head of Father Iltis, the organist, who was reflected,

B

when he sat at the manuals, in a little mirror above the organ.

Schweitzer's recollections are full of stories of this kind. The reader must go to the original text to find them in all their freshness and directness. His difficulties with Jaegli the sacristan, for instance: Jaegli's dry humour came out most notably when he tried to convince young Schweitzer, whose forehead was already abnormally protrusive, that he was growing horns, as if to renew the miracle of Moses. But the day came when he had to set off for school—apprehensively, at first— and to learn, like the others, to live with his fellows. From the beginning he wanted to be accepted by the others, who were peasants' sons, as one of them. He refused to dress like a boy from the town; and indeed his obstinacy in this respect was a great mystery to his parents. Still more typical of Schweitzer was the awakening of his sensibility, alike morally and aesthetically. In this, we can detect what came to be the basic element in his personality. His natural sympathy for the oppressed (the old Jew Mausché, for instance, whom the other boys all persecuted, and whose patience in the face of this was a lesson to young Schweitzer) and his compassion for all that lives and suffers—men and animals alike—both set him on the road of universal love: a road on which he and St Francis of Assisi walked side by side. One thing that he remembers is especially suggestive in this respect: once, when he was seven or eight years old, he went out with a friend, ostensibly to kill birds with their catapults. Not daring to refuse outright, for fear that his friend would make fun of him, young Albert held his catapult in such a way that he would be sure to miss, and so appeased his conscience.

". . . and just then the church bells rang out, mingling their chimes in the serenity of the sky with the song of the birds. It was the chime that sounded half an hour before the call to prayer. I felt as if Heaven itself were speaking to me. I threw away my catapult, scared the birds in order to put them beyond reach of my companion, and ran home as fast as I could. And now, whenever the bells ring out in the spring sky, between the bare branches, I think gratefully of the Commandment which they once, so long ago, brought home to me. Thou shalt not kill! From that day onwards, I was brave enough to emancipate myself from the fear of my fellows. Where my own deepest convictions were concerned, the opinions of others counted for nothing." The mystery of life had been revealed to a precocious spirit; it was the starting-point of Schweitzer's morality which, first founded on reverence-for-life, was to expand to the point of infinity.[1]

Schweitzer's aesthetic experience began by way of music. First there were fumbling experiments with his father's old piano, and later with the harmonium; and the intense delight of hearing "the grown-ups" sing the old songs of Alsace in two-part harmony. Music took a powerful physical hold upon the young Schweitzer. When he listened to the part-songs he trembled from head to foot and had to lean against the wall to prevent himself from falling. And when he went to his first brass-band concert he all but fainted.

When he reached the age of secondary studies, he was sent to the Lycée de Mulhouse, thanks to the

[1] A little farther on we find an identical condemnation : "Twice I went fishing with the other boys : but the way in which the worms were tortured on the hook, and the fishes' mouths were torn apart—all this filled me with such revulsion that I refused to go again."

generosity of his Uncle Louis, who was then director of the Mulhouse primary schools and had offered to take young Albert into his home for as long as he was a pupil at the Lycée. Uncle Louis and his wife, Aunt Sophie, had no children. Albert, then barely nine years old, found in their home a way of life that was regularity itself. Austere, didactic and outwardly rigorous as it may have been, it offered him an affectionate security that was to have the happiest results. At first he pined for the dear landscape of the Vosges and the Munster valley; but he found compensation in the limitless horizons of music, and these grew ever more apparent, and ever more precious.

He spent eight years in all in the Lycée de Mulhouse, and has given us a close account of his life there. Originally he was considered an unpromising pupil—so much so, in fact, that although Albert, as a pastor's son, had a small scholarship at the school, the headmaster thought seriously of having him taken away. He was "too dreamy by half". But when he found teachers who understood him, all this was changed, and he became the most brilliant of boys. In his musical studies he met with similar difficulties at the beginning, although his teacher was a man of great quality. Eugene Münch was organist at the church of St Etienne. But young Schweitzer was paralysed in his presence by timidity, or by misplaced shame, and his teacher came near to despairing of him. "It's a waste of time," he said, "to try to make you feel, if you've got no feeling in you." Albert was cut to the heart by this and made an heroic effort to master his nervousness. Once the initial confidence had been established, Eugene Münch secured results, in even a few weeks, that amazed him. Albert was overjoyed to hear that, as soon as he had been confirmed, he could begin lessons on the big organ in the church of St Etienne: this had been his dearest ambition. He had the organ in his blood and, behind him, a dynasty of pastor-organists—most notably his maternal grandfather, Pastor Schillinger, who took the keenest interest in organ-building. We can imagine with what delight the fifteen-year-old pupil first sat at the great instrument and felt his way among its three keyboards and its sixty-two stops! Before long Eugene Münch was using him as his deputy during the services, and later he took part in his master's recitals. The boy displayed, in fact, unusual intellectual precocity and, at the same time, a strong and individual talent for music. History and literature were young Albert's specialities; but, on another plane, he was equally interested in the natural sciences. Mathematics, on the other hand, left him cold. The weakly infant had given place to a strong, well-built adolescent, in whom great natural gifts were allied to an immense capacity for work. But for this last, he could not have pursued his schoolroom studies and his music at the same time; and the moral laws which had been instilled into him from childhood not only remained the basis of all his thoughts, but served to illuminate every aspect of life.

So it was that young Schweitzer came to survey his happiness and to wonder if it was right for him to accept it unthinkingly. On the one hand there were the warmth and tenderness of his family life, the satisfaction of work well done, the knowledge that the joys of music would grow ever more intense. And, on the other, the pain and suffering of the world. The consciousness of this pain had invaded Schweitzer as a child, but it had been vague and uncertain. Now that he was growing up, he began to ask himself in what way he could diminish it, however slightly, by his own direct action. A few years later, this determination was to dictate the crucial decisions of his life.

His time at the Lycée came to an end. He was just eighteen (it was 1893); his studies for the *baccalauréat* took up all his time; and he looked forward eagerly to his years at the University of Strasbourg. He passed his examination, but less brilliantly than had been expected; this was due to his differences with Albrecht, the chief examiner—though even Albrecht had to remark on his exceptional gift for history.

A new chapter in his life was about to open. His childhood was at an end. It was with real emotion that he took leave of his uncle and aunt, and of Mulhouse itself, which had once seemed so austere when compared with the freedom of Günsbach. And he went home to his parents; home, in the lovely light of a summer evening, to the warm welcome which was waiting for him in the new presbytery where his father and mother had been living since 1890. They were delighted with his successes.

It was in the autumn of that same year, 1893, while the vines of Alsace were slowly turning to gold, that Albert Schweitzer made a new friend—and one of great importance for the evolution of his gift for music and his attitude to aesthetics. In the course of a family visit to Paris, he was presented to Charles Marie Widor, the organist of St Sulpice, who was already famous both as a composer and as an executant. They made friends from the start, and their friendship grew steadily warmer. In October, however, Albert Schweitzer took up his

ary of Strasbourg. This
mas and alongside the
 are still reflected in the
scaped damage in the
ve harassed Strasbourg
s to remain for years in
at first, and later as a
enrichment in a setting
oured reflection. His
nd in theology, were
an unremitting passion
s, in fact, remained in-
ities has the sparkle of
e recently how Goethe's
 of the secrets of his
d Goethe ("two Olym-
recently called them)
r knowledge and under-
standing.

Above his desk in Günsbach, the Doctor has hung up a modestly-framed copy of a hymn which he had in his room when he was a student. It is eloquent of the fervent idealism which was then already the mark of his nature:

> Higher, ever higher,
> With your dreams and your desires,
> Higher, ever higher,
> The ideal you long to serve.
>
> Higher, ever higher,
> When the clouds begin to gather,
> Higher, ever higher,
> By the starlight of your faith.

Schweitzer has told us that it was during Whitsun-
tide, 1896, when he was barely twenty-one years old,
that he decided to spend his next ten years in the study
of science, music, and theology; and then, once he was
thirty, to give himself over completely to the service of
his fellows. The exact form of this service would become
clear to him as time went on.

Meanwhile his studies in philosophy and theology
were making rapid progress, and he had begun to learn
Hebrew, in order to read the Scriptures in the original
text. The year 1894 had been spent in compulsory
military service; but he contrived to go on with his
meditations, even when he was on manœuvres, and he
has told us how he had a Greek Testament in his pack,
and made an intensive study of the Gospel according to
St Matthew. As far as music was concerned, he had a
new friend and master in Strasbourg, in the person of
Ernest Münch, the brother of his first teacher in Mulhouse. Münch's name is still associated with the magnificent Chorale Saint-Guillaume, and two of his sons are
important figures in the world of music: Fritz Münch,
who succeeded his father as conductor of the Saint-
Guillaume choir, and Charles Münch, who began as a
violinist and is now a world-famous conductor.

Those who are fortunate enough to know Albert
Schweitzer, and to have watched him at work, can
understand how he was able to carry out a programme
of work which normally would tax the combined powers
of a group of eminent specialists. Admittedly he was
born with exceptional gifts: that inexplicable power
which we call "genius"—though the word has been too
often abused in recent years; and, with that, a constitution so powerful, and so well-balanced, that he can work

hard and continuously with no other relaxation than that which is afforded by a change in the direction of his activities. Moreover he has always striven, with crystal clarity of mind, to plan his day to the very best advantage; whether he is writing a book, or recording a Bach prelude and fugue, or carrying out a piece of medical research, or building a new part of his hospital, he prepares the ground with the same thoroughness and carries through his intentions in accordance with a carefully-meditated plan. Like Franklin, he likes to leave nothing to chance; as a child he was always day-dreaming, and as a youth his sensibility was always sending him off at a tangent, but in adult life he has become a master of method. All this, so far from diminishing the affective side of his nature, has broadened and strengthened it: and there, beyond a doubt, lies one of the secrets of his many and varied achievements.

II. THE YEARS OF STUDY. BEGINNINGS AS A WRITER AND TRAVELLER. DEPARTURE FOR AFRICA.

1897: Schweitzer was twenty-two years old.

He was finishing a thesis for his first examination in theology: "Schleiermacher's notion of the Last Supper, as compared with those of Luther, Zwingli, and Calvin." This was accepted in May 1898, and he became a scholar of the Goll Foundation. Enabled in this way to go on with his philosophical studies, he chose as his subject "Philosophy and Religion in the work of Kant". At the end of October 1898 he returned to Paris, and there studied philosophy and the organ simultaneously. He lodged at 20 Rue de la Sorbonne (not far from the Odéon Theatre, where so many of his evenings were spent). He had a quiet room on the fourth floor of an inner courtyard, and set to work in real earnest. At the Sorbonne, his teachers in the Faculty of Protestant Theology were L. H. Sabatier and L. E. Menegoz. While pursuing his work on Kant, he took organ lessons with his dear friend Widor and began also, during many conversations with the great musician, to make the first plans for his book on Bach. And he learnt the piano from two very different, but equally remarkable people: Marie Jaëll and Isidore Philipp.

Marie Jaëll, an Alsatian by birth, was destined to end her life in Alsace. She had been the disciple and the inspired friend of Liszt who, with his usual discernment, had taken the keenest interest in her many gifts. She has left certain written works which testify to the power and originality of her thought and teaching.[1]

Philipp is now a man of ninety, but he has remained wonderfully young. His influence, so long an important part of Paris university life, has more recently been widely felt in the United States. Schweitzer and he became intimate friends. But it was not easy to keep the balance between these two teachers: indeed Schweitzer records that, deeply indebted as he was to both of them, he had to play "à la Jaëll" in the morning and "à la Philipp" in the afternoon.

Schweitzer made his way with equal enthusiasm to the Bibliothéque Nationale and to St Sulpice until at last it was time to return to Strasbourg. There he showed his teacher Ziegler what progress he had made, and then he set off for Berlin, where once again he was to study music and philosophy. He lived in the most cultivated of milieux. Where philosophy was concerned, he worked mostly with Harnack, whose books he had studied at Strasbourg. Harnack remained his friend until his death in 1930. He found time to get to know the Berlin organists, and especially Professor Reimann, to whom Widor had given him an introduction. He profited greatly by this insight into the artistic and intellectual world of Berlin. He emphasises that although Paris was a universal city and the capital of its world, intellectual life in Paris was never centralised as it was in Berlin: he had never managed to penetrate to its inmost depths, as he did in Berlin.

[1] In this connection I must commend the fascinating book which Hélène Kiener, herself an Alsatian, has just written about Marie Jaëll. This book fills a deplorable gap—for has not Schweitzer said "I owe everything to that woman of genius"?

Meanwhile, at the end of July 1899, he returned to Strasbourg in order to uphold his thesis on Kant in the presence of the assembled Faculty of Letters. The thesis was published in Tübingen at the end of the same year, and helped to spread the young doctor's name (he was then only twenty-four). His teacher, Ziegler, would have liked him to take up philosophy as his profession. But Schweitzer wanted to carry on with his theology, and eventually to be able to preach. So he stayed on at Strasbourg, and was allowed to remain in the familiar environment of the seminary of St Thomas. On 1st December 1899 he was appointed pastor of St Nicholas, Strasbourg, and was to be formally established in this position after his second examination in theology. His studies centred round the atmosphere of mystery in which Jesus is enveloped. As it turned out, he had an unexpected failure in this second examination: when asked who had written a certain canticle, he replied that it had seemed to him too trifling to bother with, and that he couldn't remember. But, as luck would have it, the examiner was the son of the author in question— none other than the well-known Spitta!

At St Nicholas he was surrounded with true friends. He was entrusted with the afternoon services, the children's services, and with the teaching of doctrine: these duties suited him perfectly and allowed him to gain experience in public speaking. His sermons were prepared with immense care. Their conciseness was in fact a source of astonishment to audiences brought up on more rambling methods. He remembers one amusing instance of this: one old lady went to Pastor Knittel and complained that Schweitzer's sermons were too short, so Schweitzer asked Knittel to tell her that he was only "a poor pastor who stopped talking when he had nothing more to say".[1]

But most of his listeners were amazed and won over by his quiet, closely-packed addresses; and children listened intently, as if knowing already that they would remember his lessons for the rest of their lives. He taught them according to the doctrine of St Paul—that, when the spirit of Christ is present, the spirit of liberty must be present also. This was the foundation of his teaching, and he never wearied of the struggle against the more dogmatic, and more sterile, opinions which were then current. Schweitzer had already that power to win over the hearts and souls of fellows which has always, as I can testify from experience, been conspicuous in his nature.

He returned to Paris—anxious, as always, to see Widor again. And he made new friends, who included Romain Rolland, with whom he was later to be less perfectly in accord, and Henri Lichtenberger, whose profound knowledge of German literature won Schweitzer's admiration. During the summer of 1900 he visited Bavaria, where he went to see the legendary Passion Play at Oberammergau. The actors' infectious fervour moved him, despite the banality of both text and music. As is well known, every actor in the play is, and has been for centuries, an inhabitant of Oberammergau itself. Next he made a pilgrimage to Bayreuth and renewed his acquaintance with Cosima Wagner, who had already made a deep impression upon him at Strasbourg, and with her son Siegfried, whose artistic energies and generosity

---

[1] In preparing his books, Schweitzer has kept to this same method. That is to say he first writes out the text at length; then he revises it with great care, and gradually cuts it until he has put the maximum of substance into the minimum number of pages.

of heart quite conquered Schweitzer. Both became close friends. At Bayreuth he also met Houston Stewart Chamberlain, the husband of Eva Wagner; but the tendencies of this formidable intellect later brought him into direct opposition to Schweitzer. (As is well known, Chamberlain's ideas upon racial problems were similar to those of Gobineau, and in fact went farther upon the same lines. He had none the less been an aesthetician of the first order.) All this took place, of course, on the "sacred hill", where the atmosphere of musical mysticism was intense. Schweitzer had always been a Wagnerian (a performance of *Tannhäuser* at Mulhouse had come to him as an overwhelming revelation) and he is still a convinced and outspoken enthusiast for the master. This we may judge from the letter which he sent in 1951 to Siegfried Wagner's sons, Wieland and Wolfgang, on the occasion of the reopening of the Festival Theatre at Bayreuth.

His studies of theology and history brought him back to the question of the Last Supper and the "historical Jesus". In 1900 he took his *licence* in theology with a thesis on the "Problem of the Last Supper, as it emerges from the studies and researches of the nineteenth century". In 1902 a second thesis, on Christ's Messianic ideas, won him an appointment as *maître des conférences*. And from 1901 to 1912, he fulfilled this function in the Faculty of Protestant Theology, while carrying on at the same time with his private researches. But, at the same time, two important "intermezzi", as he himself calls them, began to run parallel to, though quite outside, his university activities. The first of these was nothing less than the preparation and composition of his book on *Bach, the musician-poet*, which his master Widor had

asked him to undertake. This turned out, as we all
know, to be a masterpiece; the first edition was published in 1905, in Paris, by Costallat. The second
"intermezzo" was his decision to study medicine: its
repercussions were to affect the whole course of his
life.

As has been said, Schweitzer gave himself ten years,
as from Whitsun 1896, to study as he wished—music,
philosophy, and theology: thenceforward, he was to
shape his life, once and for all, as a contribution to the
struggle against evil and suffering. In 1904 he read an
article in the Paris *Journal des Missions Evangéliques*,
and this revived the spring of inner sympathy which had
welled up within him when first he saw Bartholdi's
figure of the negro in the Bruat monument at Colmar.
Suddenly he realised where his path was to lie. Poverty
and suffering were rampant in Equatorial Africa. Whole
tribes were being ravaged by sleeping sickness. Missionaries and teachers and doctors were urgently needed.
Schweitzer resolved to begin studying medicine forthwith. On 13th October 1906 he posted a number of
letters—to his parents and his closest friends—from a
box in the Avenue de la Grande Armée; these announced his decision to take up medicine, and to leave as
soon as possible for Equatorial Africa. The stupefaction,
and indeed the indignation, of his academic friends in
Strasbourg and Berlin can readily be imagined. Widor
did his best to deter him; Schweitzer was already famous at thirty; he was known as a philosopher and a
theologian, and very soon he would be known also as a
musician. How could he throw up all this and go off
into the jungle? It would, at best, be an uncertain, un-
dependable adventure; and there were others who were

free to go, and would risk nothing of what Schweitzer was risking.

Nothing could shake him; his decision was based upon absolute moral values. He explained this with his usual lucidity; till then, he had written and spoken: now it was time to act—time to put the religion of love to the test of reality: the tests of the pulpit and the examination-room were no longer sufficient. In 1906 he became a student of the Strasbourg Faculty of Medicine.

I have heard him speak of the painful struggles which all this involved. "Theology and music," he said, "were more or less natural languages to me. I came of a long line of pastors and organists, and I had grown up in an atmosphere of music and theology. But medicine! That was a different world, and I was quite unprepared for it. Often I used to come out of my medical classes and go straight to St Guillaume, where I found Ernest Münch. And after an hour of Bach—oh, the healing power of that man! I calmed down again, and got back my equilibrium."

For seven years Schweitzer worked as a medical student: but they were years in which music and theology continued to take up much of his time. Incredible as it would seem, to anyone who did not know how rigorously Schweitzer disciplines the use of his time, he published several important books during those seven years. He also mastered the technique of organ-building, re-wrote his *J. S. Bach* for the German edition, and at twice the length of the previous version written in French, and gave a great many concerts—notably in Paris, where he was organist of the Bach Society, in company with his friend Gustave Bret.

Up till 1912 he went on with his work as lecturer in

the Faculty of Protestant Theology, and as pastor at St Nicholas. He was especially attached to St Nicholas. In 1906 he brought out the first edition of his *The Quest of the Historical Jesus*. The first version of this bore the sub-title *From Reimarus to Wrede*. He did, in fact, include a study and comparison of the *Lives* of Reimarus, the famous Hamburg orientalist (1694–1798), and of Venturini, Strauss, Renan, Keim, etc. He also surveyed the work of Harnack, Colani, Volkmar, and Wrede, which had appeared five years previously, in 1901. Wrede died in 1907; he had the highest opinion of Schweitzer's work. *The Quest* was translated into English in 1910, and has had as great a success in England as in Germany: its influence has been as far-reaching, moreover, in Catholic as in Protestant circles.

In this same year, 1906, he began at Bayreuth ("after a marvellous performance of *Tristan*," he tells us, "and in my room at the Black Horse Inn") the German version of his *J. S. Bach*. Originally a book of 445 pages, it ended up with nearly twice as many. And, again in 1906, he published his comparative study of French and German organ-building. He also went on with his fight for the preservation of old organs, and against the new tendency of organ-builders to concentrate on volume and on novel sonorities at the expense of beauty and purity of sound. He came out strongly in praise and defence of the great French builder Cavaillé-Coll; in 1909, at the Vienna International Congress, he secured the adoption of his "General Regulations for Organ-Builders", which were afterwards published in several languages and did a great deal of good. In the chapter of his autobiography which is devoted to the organ, he

C

recalls how his friends said of him: "In Africa he saves old niggers, in Europe old organs."

He tells us, too, that more than once the struggle for the old organs was so difficult and so exasperating that he wondered if he would not have done better never to take it up. But there is no curing so generous a passion; even in 1952 he had no sooner reached Alsace than he set off at the first mention of an organ that needed to be rescued or put in repair.

Schweitzer's "grand design" dates from the moment, nearly fifty years ago, when his books began to sell, and his concerts and lectures to attract big audiences, and he could begin to put aside the money for his hospital. For he had decided to build and equip a hospital in a particularly forbidding part of the jungle. His gifts and his energies were so varied that he could make the service of Beauty and the Ideal go to work in the service of reality. And there were many with every year that passed, throughout Europe, in Switzerland and Holland as much as in France and in Germany, in every country where Schweitzer became known as a lecturer and an organist, who asked of their own accord to be allowed to take part in his adventure. (Later, committees were formed of "Friends of Lambaréné"; in Britain, Switzerland, Holland, Scandinavia, Germany, France and the U.S.A. These were able to form collecting centres, and in this way to help to extend and amplify the hospital's work.)

How did the hard-working medical student contrive to go on with his triple career? The question comes to us naturally, as we watch his activity during those seven years. In Paris he not only saw his older friends, but made new ones as well: the Theodore Reinachs and

Comtesse Mélanie de Pourtalès (through whom he
came to know Princess Metternich who, in her youth, as
wife of the Austrian Ambassador to Paris, had been one
of the earliest and most prominent of Wagnerians). In
Spain, he played in Madrid before the King and Queen;
in Barcelona he made friends with Luis Milet, the
director of the Orfeo Catala (his son, like himself an
admirable musician, later succeeded him at the head of
this fine choir), and with other Catalans. Eventually he
returned to Günsbach where, together with his parents,
he found the friends of his boyhood, talked once again
with the farmers and the men of the vineyards, and went
off to meditate on the rocky heights overlooking the
valley. (The commune was later to offer him, in a
moving act of homage, the site of these early meditations.)

In 1906, now that *The Quest of the Historical Jesus* had
appeared, he turned with equal ardour to study the rôle
and the thought of St Paul. His researches extended
to every volume that had appeared on the subject since
the seventeenth century. Grotius's *Annotations on the
New Testament* was the pioneer among them. In 1911
Schweitzer published his *Paul and His Interpreters*;
likewise in 1911 there appeared the first volumes of his
working edition of Bach's organ works. He had worked
on this continuously, with Widor, who had paid many
visits to Günsbach where they had worked quietly
together in the peace of the Alsatian countryside.

In 1912, and not without a great sadness in his heart,
Schweitzer resigned his posts as pastor and lecturer.
On 18th June he was married to Hélène Bresslau, the
daughter of Professor Bresslau, director of historical
studies at Strasbourg University. He and his fiancée had

long enjoyed the closest intimacy in the world of ideas. He had known Hélène Bresslau when she was a student, she had known every detail of his projects, and she took an intense delight in all that he did; it was with her that he had decided to set off on his African adventure.

He returned to Paris, in order to complete his medical studies with a special course of colonial medicine; and also to document himself further for the journey and the installation of his hospital. He gave concerts—notably with the Bach Society of Paris—and so enabled himself to pay for the printing of his medical thesis. He had chosen a subject which derived from his earlier studies and yet allowed him to make a new contribution to knowledge, *The Psychiatric Study of Jesus.*

The problems of his departure were by no means resolved. He had chosen to build his hospital at Lambaréné on the River Ogowe, in the centre of a tropical forest. The Lambaréné mission had been set up in 1876 by American missionaries. When the Gabon became a French colony, in 1892, it had become attached to the Société des Missions de Paris. But Albert Schweitzer was, in law, a German citizen, and his medical diplomas had been granted by the Faculty of Strasbourg, which at that time was a German city. Therefore he had to secure authority to practise medicine in French territory. His friends in Paris intervened on his behalf, and the matter was settled satisfactorily. But new obstacles arose when he approached the Société des Missions. His powerful personality was already familiar there; the novelty of some of his theological views had struck fear into several members of the committee. They invited him to appear before them and justify his opinions. He refused; but he did go to see them, one by one, and he

won them all over by his evident sincerity. In the end
it was he who imposed his conditions—to the amazement of many people in Paris: he refused to accept any
salary, explaining that his *J. S. Bach* and other books
and his recitals had made enough money for his basic
expenses. And he made it quite clear that his African
activities were to be exclusively medical. Where theology was concerned he would, he assured them, be
"silent as a carp". This assurance removed any lingering
objections. Not another moment was lost: the Doctor
and his wife completed the packing of the many boxes
in which were stowed their medical supplies and indispensable provisions. Seventy such boxes were sent to
Bordeaux by February 1913. Schweitzer decided to take
in addition a supply of gold equivalent, in to-day's
values, to several hundreds of pounds. When his wife
asked him why he was doing this, he replied that un-
fortunately they had to reckon with the possibility of
war. In such a case, banknotes might become worthless,
but gold would never lose its value.

Things were going badly in the Europe of 1913.
Neither the French nor the German people wanted war,
and in Europe there was still a chance of peace; but in
the Slav countries uncertainty had reached a point of
almost theatrical tension. The Doctor's apprehensions
were all too well founded; and they weighed heavily
upon him. He nevertheless devoted his whole strength
to the project for which he had striven so long. It was
on Good Friday 1913 that he and his wife left Günsbach
—not without deep feeling, but buoyed up with hopes
that knew no bounds. Schweitzer has told us what it
meant to him to hear, on that day, the bells that had
rung out throughout his childhood and adolescence.

And, as a fanatical enthusiast for Bayreuth, he was (as he told me himself) struck by the coincidence which caused him to leave on the day that Wagner has evoked with such magical effect in *Parsifal*.

At Strasbourg there were, once again, the most heartfelt of farewells. Then on to Paris, where on Easter Day his dear friend Widor brought out every nuance of the great organ which had so long been dear to Schweitzer's heart. In the early afternoon they took the train from the Gare d'Orsay to Bordeaux. Schweitzer still remembers the wonderful weather in which they travelled to south-western France. And the sunshine on the port of Bordeaux, which was to become so familiar to him; and the sunlit decks of the vessel in which the young couple installed themselves and their great hopes. It was in this sunlight of high promise that the *Europe* sailed on 20th March 1913 for the open sea: for Africa: and for the Unknown which, on the line of the Equator, awaits those whose hands and hearts are heavy-laden with faith and with love.

III. LAMBARÉNÉ. THE WAR OF 1914. THE FIRST RETURN TO EUROPE.

On this boat there is a passenger in whom we are particularly interested. His tall silhouette is outlined in the bows. Let us look closely at him. Schweitzer is thirty-eight years old: physically he is in his prime. He is a big man, broad-shouldered, built solidly and built to last. His face has been moulded and marked by life: the lofty brow—a noble dome, within which the innumerable thoughts are quickly set in order—the emphatic nose, and what we can see of the mouth, beneath the heavy moustaches: all reveal an immense loving-kindness. There is great energy in the chin. The brown hair is thrown backwards; its crest is unruly. But it is above all the eyes which are unforgettable—for their tender authority and the pellucid gaze that penetrates and holds you captive. Schweitzer's face has been compared to Nietszche's; but the resemblance is entirely external. The unruly hair and drooping moustaches alone justify it. Nietszche's face was narrower and sharper; you could see from it that he was unbalanced. Schweitzer's is broad, and breaks naturally into the most kindly of smiles.

With the years, his features will become more deeply marked, and his hair and moustaches will whiten, but the uniquely-recognisable mask will never lose its luminous power. The cast of his features is very characteristic of his native Alsace. The Doctor has remained faithful to his black suit, his high wing collar, and the

white shirt with its black bow tie: they are the clothes
of a doctor and a pastor, and only in Africa do they give
place to the indispensable suit of white linen.

His hands are no less remarkable than his face: they
are large, certainly, but well-shaped. The impression
they leave is one both of strength and of subtlety: and
of infinite expressiveness. They are hands which can
attempt anything and succeed in anything. Pen, pencil,
scalpel and bandage—all come naturally to them, with
an identical lightness and precision. The builder's hammer and saw are at home in these hands, and at the
keyboard of the organ they become as eloquent as the
voice of a Caruso. How many portraits have been made
of Schweitzer! Drawings, oil-paintings, busts, medal-
lions and medals—one day his iconography will be
compiled. Some are very fine; but none, I think, so
revealing as the amazing series of photographs which
show him at Lambaréné, at Günsbach, in Paris, and elsewhere. Erica Anderson, an artist with the camera, has
made a varied collection of these, and beyond Schweitzer's
physical appearance they reveal his inner being.

One thing more, and our sketch is finished. Albert
Schweitzer's handwriting has not changed since he was
a young man. It is a handwriting like no other; small,
erect, perfectly legible; graphologists delight in it. The
Doctor once told me that some Swiss friends had his
handwriting analysed—without, of course, saying whose
it was. "The graphologist was very kind," he said.
"He said a lot of nice things about me . . . But at the
end he said 'There's a marked despotic tendency'." And
Schweitzer turned to me with that pure and resonant
laugh which his friends know so well and said "Well,
what d'you think of that?" I said that the graphologist

was quite right; for I thought, and I still think, that a man who bears a message must have the gift of authority —an authority that all will acknowledge, if his message be true. In every apostle, a born leader lies hid.

Back to the boat. The weather changed, that day in March 1913, almost as soon as the *Europe* got out to the open sea. Brilliant sunshine gave place to fog; and fog gave portent of a storm. On the second day out, the storm broke, and the poor *Europe* pitched and tossed on the riotous Atlantic. The Schweitzers, in their in-experience, had not stowed their baggage properly, and it all went careering to and fro across their cabin. Even the cooks couldn't stand upright in front of their ovens, so that only cold food could be served. All this lasted for three days—an eternity, as it seemed to the pas-sengers: but at last they drew near to Teneriffe. Schweitzer didn't want to miss the famous apparition of the snow-capped peak that towers above that island. But he admits to having been so tired out by the voyage that he didn't wake up till they were actually inside the harbour of Santa Cruz.

With the return of good weather, the passengers were at last able to make friends with one another. Most of them were Army officers, military doctors, and colonial civil servants. He talked with some of them, notably with a military doctor who had already spent a dozen years in Equatorial Africa; from him he learnt things of great value, especially from the bacteriological point of view. And, now that the sun was directly overhead, everybody dressed in white and wore the colonial helmets that were then thought to be an indispensable protection against sunstroke.

Dakar: for the first time Doctor and Madame

Schweitzer set foot on the continent to which they hoped
to devote their lives. The sight of so many ill-treated
animals gave a new twist to their feelings; the Doctor's
Franciscan heart was deeply wounded by their sufferings
and he at once tried to intervene, while the "old colo-
nials" looked on sceptically. There is no doubt (I know
it myself, from what I have seen in Morocco) that all
too many Africans are extremely and continuously
brutal in their treatment of animals. The little donkeys
are martyred, and as the emaciated horses drag their
heavy loads along the street, the harness bites into their
bleeding sides and the driver cuts at the sores with his
pointed stick. Albert Schweitzer's feelings, when he
first saw these things, can readily be imagined. He did
all he could to remedy this unpromising state of affairs;
and his example was surprisingly effective.

Dakar, Conakry. Sharks played in the wake of the
Europe, and at each port of call natives dived for coins
that the passengers tossed down into the harbour. The
boat gradually emptied; it grew hotter; each evening a
storm swept across the sky on the port side, where the
coast was never far away. Sunday 13th April: their
last stop: the Schweitzers were delighted by the happy
faces of the blacks who had come to the American
Mission service. And on the 14th they reached Port-
Gentil, where the formidable customs examination
awaited them, and they spent their last night on board
ship.

The *Alembé*, the river steamer on which the Doctor
was to sail up the Ogowe, appeared to date from the
pre-history of steamship design. Its two paddle-wheels
were situated astern, to avoid floating tree-trunks. Once
they were past the estuary of the Ogowe, they found

themselves in a typical equatorial landscape: the broad
river, the virgin forest running down to, and over, the
banks, the monkeys hanging from palm-trees, and the
indecipherable tangle of roots and lianas in which animals beyond number lay hidden. The Ogowe was not
one stream but many. Some were as broad as lakes;
others, like narrow canals. The Doctor was interested
to see how many native huts were lying derelict. When
he asked why this was, he was told that these were poor
villages which had once been prosperous, but were now
abandoned. "But why?" Almost in a whisper came the
answer: "Brandy." And the boat went on its ghostly,
moonlit way until midnight.

The forest became more mysterious, and more hos-
tile, as they paddled deeper and deeper into Africa.
Suddenly a hand pointed out to the Doctor and his wife
some hills in the distance. "Lambaréné!" Schweitzer
gazed intently at the horizon which he was to know so
well. Towards four o'clock they reached the landing-
stage, and there they had an agreeable surprise. The
two missionaries had come to meet them. (The mission
station was an hour away, by canoe.) And with them
were the children who attended their two classes. The
Schweitzers and their luggage were transferred without
mishap to the canoes, and the youthful boatmen bore
them off at top speed. At the mission station there was
another warm reception, and the little house which was
to be the Schweitzers' had been decorated and hung
with flowers. It was a wooden house, built on iron
stakes. The view stretched across the river, the forest,
and a blue line of mountains in the distance. Night fell,
like a shutter; and with it there came a chorus of sound
that went straight to the Schweitzers' hearts.

And so Dr Schweitzer began his first visit to Lambaréné. It was to last for four years—till 1917, when it was interrupted by the necessities of the first World War. The Doctor has described it himself. In his usual spare, precise, deliberately objective style he has written of several important episodes in this first sojourn. During those four years he put at the disposal of the mission not only his spiritual energies, but also every ounce of his physical strength. He cut and cleared trees. He prepared the stockades. He planned the huts and built them with his own hands. And all this in the midst of innumerable problems. These problems—and they were never the same—were of many kinds. Many arose from the difficulty of working with savages who had no notion at all of method and continuity, as we understand them; there was also the struggle against Nature— vegetable Nature, animal Nature, insect Nature. The heat was gruelling throughout. And there were disappointments of every sort, mercifully tempered by the knowledge that they were doing necessary work and relieving the sufferings of others. Something that brought him great joy was the graceful action of the Paris Bach Society who, wishing to thank their organist, had made him a present of a piano fitted with organ-pedals. This had reached Lambaréné after great difficulties, and in the evenings the Doctor could resume his Bach or improvise as he wished.

The original "hospital" was simply an old fowls'-house beside their hut, which they had cleaned and whitewashed. But it was too small. The canvas hut which Schweitzer had had in mind proved very hard to build, and it was only in November that they could begin to equip it. Two weeks later it was in use. A waiting-room came next, and then a barn-like erection which was meant for the in-patients who had hitherto been dumped in the boathouse. Not a day passed without something being enlarged, or improved, or re-equipped.

Meanwhile there was very intensive medical activity. Schweitzer notes that he treated nearly 2,000 patients during his first nine months at Lambaréné, although they began with only the barest necessities for their work. Surgical operations were performed by the Doctor in the open air in front of the house, with Madame Schweitzer as his assistant. They were successful, though some were very serious; this soon spread his fame, and the natives, for whom the idea of recovery is indissolubly linked with that of fetishism, became convinced of his healing powers. Therein lay a question of profound importance, which Schweitzer studied over and over again: for those who believe in fetishes and magical powers are naturally terrified of evil spells. They live in terror of evil spirits, and of the maleficent influences which overshadow every moment of life on earth.

Doctor Schweitzer, still faithful to the law of absolute reverence for life, refused to go fishing or hunting for pleasure. He took life only when absolutely necessary, which astonished many of his fellow-whites and dumbfounded the natives. He constantly put into action the admirable precept which occurs in his *Civilisation and Ethics*. "Ethics", he said, "are *respect for life*—where that respect extends to infinity." And, a little farther on, there is this corresponding passage: "before I harm a living creature, of no matter what kind, I must carefully examine whether or not my action is inevitable."

In July 1914 the Doctor could take stock of his position and rejoice. The hospital buildings were already quite extensive. They were properly arranged and equipped. Surgical operations could be carried out in more or less normal conditions. Patients could be accepted, and looked after, in ever greater numbers. But the outbreak of war in August of that year had the worst possible repercussions upon the work of the hospital. Any further expansion was out of the question. Albert Schweitzer and his wife were German citizens, in law; and in Lambaréné they were treated as such. They could stay on in their house, but were allowed no communication with the outer world. They were under continual surveillance. These measures betoken an almost incredible lack of discernment on the part of the authorities; but the Schweitzers rose superior to injustice. Deprived of all means of helping their fellow-creatures directly, they set themselves new objectives in the life of the spirit—in philosophy, in theology, and in music. When Widor learned of their predicament, he protested violently, and to such effect that the authorities consented to modify the terms of their imprisonment. Schweitzer resumed his medical activity. His native patients had never been able to understand why the colonial authorities should have treated the Doctor so strangely: magic, they thought, had been his only offence.

The war went on. In September 1917 there was another painful episode. The Clémenceau government, bent only on hastening the end of the war, tightened its precautions against all those who had been born in countries with whom France was at war. Alsatians, as usual, were the first to suffer. And the Schweitzers were consigned to an internment camp in France itself. They had only an hour or two in which to pack, as best they could, their instruments, medicines, and equipment, and lock them away in one of the huts. The Doctor was allowed to take with him the draft of his *Philosophy of Civilisation*, the fruit for the most part of the dark days of the war. The Father Superior of the Catholic Mission came to say good-bye, in terms which revealed a touching gratitude, and said that they hoped soon to see him back again. This was not to be, for shortly after the end of the war the Father was returning to Europe in the *Afrique* (which had also carried the Schweitzers back to France) when the ship sank with all hands in the Bay of Biscay.

On the voyage back to France Schweitzer was not allowed to speak to the other passengers, so he decided to learn some Bach fugues and Widor's Sixth Symphony by heart. One morning, the estuary of the Gironde came into view; the scene that they had gazed upon, four years earlier, when leaving for Africa.

For the next three months they were shut up in a barracks in Bordeaux. Then they moved, in winter, to the disaffected convent of Garaison in the Pyrenees. It was cold there, and there was an amazing medley of internees: Schweitzer the doctor and Schweitzer the psychologist found among them many a case for compassionate study. In the spring it was decided to move him to St Rémy, in Provence. This at least had a milder climate; and, as it turned out, a milder discipline. The Doctor recognised in his surroundings the subject of a painting by Van Gogh. He was, in fact, in the asylum in which Van Gogh had lived and worked! But the mistral had a bad effect upon the Schweitzers, whose health by then was none too sound, and after lengthy negotiations their friends in Paris succeeded in arranging for them to be taken to the Swiss frontier in July 1918. They were warmly received in Switzerland, and after a time they were able to continue their journey to Alsace. War-time conditions compelled the train to stop at Colmar, and it was on foot that the Doctor climbed the valley towards the home that he had left on Good Friday 1913. The carillons had given place to gunfire: the battle of the Vosges was being carried on within earshot of Günsbach. Yet life in the valley went on much as usual, despite the continual risk of bombardment. Schweitzer returned to Strasbourg, where he was taken on at the Municipal Hospital and allowed to resume his duties as Pastor of St Nicholas. But he had no news from Lambaréné, and could hope for none; and it can be imagined how often his thoughts carried him thither.

When the Armistice at last put an end to the tragedy, one of his first thoughts was to go and help those of his German friends who were destitute. He wanted, too, to see his family and his friends in France. Gradually he unshackled his mind from the painful limitations which had been imposed upon him; and his constitution, so long jeopardised by privation and internment, began to pick up again. Soon he had all his old appetite for work, and for the philosopher, the musician, and the lecturer, the years 1918–24 were exceptionally fruitful.

On 14th January 1919 Madame Schweitzer brought into the world their daughter Rhena. Schweitzer himself, though busy with the double duties of a doctor and a pastor, and still deprived of the manuscripts which he had had to leave at Lambaréné, decided to fill in his time with an elaborate new scheme of research— nothing less than a comparative study of the great reli-

gions: Judaism, Christianity, Islam, the cult of Zara-
thustra, Brahmanism, Buddhism, Chinese mysticism.
He was delighted, meanwhile, with the warmth of his
reception in Barcelona, which he had revisited as organist for the Orfeo Catala.

A few days before Christmas, Schweitzer received a
letter of invitation from Archbishop Söderblom, the head
of the Protestant Church of Sweden and a famous theologian. Would he come to Uppsala and give a series of
lectures for the Olaus-Petri foundation? Schweitzer was
pleased and surprised. He had come, he tells us, to
consider himself as "a coin that had rolled under a ward-
robe and been forgotten". The journey to Barcelona
had given him new strength, and the invitation from
Uppsala touched him deeply. His lectures were delivered
in an atmosphere which proved to him, once and for all,
that he was not forgotten by those who had shown him
their confidence in 1913. His stay in Sweden completed
his rehabilitation, both physically and morally. His concerts were so successful that he was able to pay off his
long-standing debts, notably to the Société des Missions
and to certain of his friends in Paris. When he left
Sweden in the summer of 1920 he knew, to his great
delight, that he would be able to return to Lambaréné,
and to take up once again the work which had been so
brutally interrupted.

We cannot here follow in detail the story of his
travels and his manifold activities. When he passed
through Switzerland, his lectures and concerts were followed with passionate enthusiasm; in 1920 he was
given an honorary doctorate by Zurich University. In
the same year was first published, in Sweden, his account
of the building of his hospital which has become famous

D

as *On the Edge of the Primeval Forest* and has been translated into many languages. Quite apart from its lively and invaluable description of the hospital itself, the book comprised several important essays: on the problem of illness among the natives, and its moral implications, and also on the responsibility of civilisation towards backward peoples. The book had, on every page, that profound, reverberating humanity which is the foundation of everything that Schweitzer writes and does.

In 1921 Schweitzer paid further visits to both Sweden and Switzerland. He was welcomed everywhere. In 1922 he lectured at Oxford, Birmingham, Cambridge, and in London, on the religious problems which are nearest his heart: Christianity and the religions of the world, and the question of St Paul. He gave more and more organ recitals. But the summer of 1922 was devoted to his *Philosophy of Civilisation*, and for this he spent most of his time in his family home at Günsbach, with occasional visits to Strasbourg, where he stayed with either his friends the Dietzes, or with M. Kuntz, the President of the Reformed Church.

In 1923 he was for a time in Prague, and became a friend of Professor Oskar Kraus, the faithful disciple of Brentano. He stopped off at Bayreuth to pay his respects to Cosima Wagner and to give her a bouquet of roses. He also revisited his other friends there. On his return he brought out his masterwork *Civilisation and Ethics*. It appeared first in Munich, in German, and then in English. In its last chapter he argued with vehemence that only the ethical conception of reverence-for-life could arrest the dramatic decline of our civilisation. While revising and correcting the proofs, he was packing his boxes for the return to Lambaréné. For he was being continually begged to return there; people were waiting for him; there was no other doctor; he was badly needed. He didn't hesitate. He contrived, though, to keep everything going at once: the publication of his book *Christianity and the Religions of the World*; the minutely-detailed preparations for his departure; the writing of his childhood memories (which appeared soon after and were translated into many languages). These memoirs, so fresh and so simple, are of great importance for those who wish to understand Schweitzer and his work. They arose from a conversation which Schweitzer had, in the late summer of 1923, with Dr Pfister, the Zurich psycho-analyst. Dr Pfister had made notes of this conversation, in which Schweitzer had talked for two hours about the first twenty years of his life.

But Dr Schweitzer could not linger over the past. Box after box of medicines had to be got ready, his equipment needed to be reviewed, and there were formalities to be completed. In the end Madame Schweitzer had to stay behind in Europe with little Rhena. She was still by no means well. Noel Gillespie, a young Oxford student of medicine and chemistry, went out with the Doctor. His previous experience made it possible for Schweitzer to have only what was absolutely essential in his luggage, and to have it packed in the right way. On 14th February 1924 he once again said "Au revoir" to his native country, his parents' home, and his dear ones. Gillespie met him at Bordeaux; and Schweitzer set off on his second African experiment. Once again he did not hesitate to give up all that Europe could offer, although he had not merely recaptured but considerably extended his triple reputation as a musician, a theologian and a philosopher.

IV. AFRICA AND EUROPE. THE SECOND WORLD WAR. THE PRESENT.

They travelled in a Dutch cargo-boat, the *Orestes*, and reached Port-Gentil after an unexpected stop in the Cameroons. We can imagine the Doctor's feelings when he sighted, first the equatorial horizon, then Cape Lopez, and then Port-Gentil. He was deeply moved, too, by the welcome which greeted him when "the Gabon's own doctor" stepped ashore. Three days' journey upstream: thirteen years had passed since he first set sail, with his young wife, on the Ogowe. The country seemed unchanged; but when they got to Lambaréné the hospital was in ruins, the roofs had fallen in, and the walls were collapsing. But blacks and whites alike gave Schweitzer so pathetically warm a welcome that he could not but draw fresh hope from it. That very day he got down to work. Axe, hammer, and saw came into action. But there was also urgent medical work to be done; for hundreds of miles round, the tom-toms had spread the news of the "Big Doctor's" return. More food had to be got, and the roofs needed repairing. There were a thousand things to be done. And Gillespie would soon have to leave for England.

Fortunately there arrived in July, 1924, a young nurse from Strasbourg, Mathilde Kottmann. She became, and remained, one of the keystones of the whole edifice. In October the party was reinforced by the arrival of an Alsatian doctor, Dr Nessmann. The hospital buildings were restored, enlarged and improved in every way. The Doctor had, however, to overcome the incomprehension of several tribes which had been newly transferred to the region to work for the timber trade. It needed endless patience to circumvent the dangerous situations which might have arisen from this. In 1925 a new doctor, a Swiss from Berne, Dr Lauterbourg, came to strengthen the team. He was an experienced surgeon and freed Schweitzer to devote some of his time to the exhausting but indispensable work of building and equipping new huts. On 5th May 1925, Pastor Schweitzer died in his home at Günsbach. He was more than eighty years old, but to the end he had followed his son's manifold apostolate with the keenest enthusiasm.

Autumn 1925. A new nurse from Strasbourg, Emma Haussknecht, arrived in her turn. Her devotion was to make of her one of the Doctor's most faithful assistants, still to-day a tower of strength at Lambaréné. The European personnel of the hospital now numbered five: the work could be shared out quite rationally, and everything promised well. But an appalling epidemic of amoebic dysentery suddenly multiplied the number of patients to a point at which the hospital appeared far too small. Nor could it be enlarged; the river on one side, and its tributaries on the other, put that out of the question.

The Doctor then made a vital decision: to look for a new site, and on that site to build a new hospital. First he had to be allotted a site large enough for the construction of a great many hutments, with an isolation ward, fields, and a kitchen garden. Next, there would have to be material assistance from his friends in Europe. He couldn't do without it, and it would have to come soon. All this came about, as if by a miracle. The hill was chosen, and the site cleared and made ready, and in a few weeks building began. This time the huts were all of considerable size, wooden-beamed, with timber-walls and canvas roofs. Each was raised on stakes, so that the floor was a yard from the ground. Schweitzer not only supervised every detail of the work, but took part in it himself. His long experience proved invaluable. Gradually the hospital took on the air of an entire village—some forty buildings. It was dominated by the in-patients' ward, which stood higher than the Doctor's own house. Meanwhile, patients were still being treated in the old hospital. Dr Nessmann had returned to Europe and was replaced by Dr Frédéric Trensz of Strasbourg, who later displayed exceptional gifts in the field of colonial medicine. New nurses came out from England and Switzerland. There was more and more work; communications between the two sites were made very much easier by the generosity of the Swedes, who presented Schweitzer with a motor pinnace.

On 21st January 1927 the move was completed and the Doctor, radiant in spite of his fatigue, made the round of the new hospital. Everybody was delighted, and looked it. During the following months the Doctor was constantly perfecting, completing, and improving the new organisation. The services of medicine and surgery were grouped in the centre building; the whole hospital could, at that time, house 250 patients. But there were also their families: the total complement rose in this way to nearly 600 persons. Plans for isolating infectious patients were now ready; and as for the treatment of lepers, we shall presently see on what a scale this was to develop.

Dr Trensz had to return to Alsace, but in March 1927 Dr Mundler came out in his stead. The medical team, both male and female, was now complete; and there was some first-class material among the African contingent. Schweitzer could therefore afford to plan an overdue and necessary visit to Europe. Everything was made ready, and on 21st July he left Lambaréné. He could not but feel a bitter pang as he sailed away from the continent which had become his second country and away, too, from his colleagues, and from the African patients to whom he was so deeply attached.

He was very happy to find his wife and daughter installed at Königsfeld, in the Black Forest. Faithful friends flocked to greet him. But his father's death had robbed him of the place where it was easiest to work and easiest to relax, the memory-haunted presbytery of Günsbach. His life took on its usual many-sided intensity; his heart belonged to Lambaréné, and his thoughts also, but he turned back to his lectures, his recitals, and the books which he had long planned to complete. In the autumn he went to Sweden. And from there to Denmark, where music, philosophy, and theology were his concerns. And meanwhile, in the Rue des Greniers, a street in the heart of old Strasbourg, he organised a sort of "G.H.Q." for the sorting and dispatch of the presents that flowed in on their way to Lambaréné. With his devoted and incomparable helpers, Emmy Martin and Pastor Woytt, he soon had this working with ideal simplicity. Madame Martin became the guiding spirit of an organisation which had its links not only with Africa, but with every country in Europe, and soon, indeed, with the whole world. Schweitzer had a room there—a veritable cell—and to the legs of his work-table he tied two sacks: one of letters that needed attention, the other of letters that had already been answered. The sacks of answered letters, when full, were tied up, labelled, and stored away. His correspondence already extended to every part of the globe.

His travels took him to Holland, England, Czechoslovakia, Paris: an international fraternity arose among those who, in every country in Europe, were following his work. He delayed the completion of the final draft of his *Mysticism of Paul the Apostle* to go to Frankfurt and receive the Goethe Prize for "his general services to humanity". His profound knowledge of Goethe's work and personality enabled him to range far and wide in his address of thanks, and to make powerful affirmation of his own faith in idealism and in the principle of reverence-for-life.

With the money which the Prize had brought him, Schweitzer decided to build a house at Günsbach. In this way—assuming that he ever allowed himself the leisure—he could recapture the cherished environment of his childhood. He chose the site, a little way outside the village, and drew up the plans himself; his experience at Lambaréné had made him a perfectly competent architect. And so it was that there arose, on the edge of the road to Munster, the house in which I have often had the great happiness of being a guest. Simple convenience is the keynote of everything in this plainest of houses. I shall never forget my first visit there: and how the Doctor showed me the young vines he had trained across the façade. "You see!" he said laughingly, "This is Monsieur Goethe's house. It's thanks to him that I've been able to build it." In point of fact, however, Schweitzer refused to use the prize money for his own advantage until he had raised, and given to charity, an equivalent sum in fees for lectures and recitals.

He returned to Czechoslovakia to receive an honorary doctorate in Prague. Germany came next, and then Switzerland. The Swiss had always been particularly sensitive to the Doctor's apostolate: not only had they given very generously to his funds, but there had always been a Swiss, whether male or female, among the volunteers at Lambaréné. In the summer of 1929, Schweitzer made ready to return to Africa; and this time Madame Schweitzer was to go with him. He felt, and in fact he knew, that he was needed there. On Boxing Day he left for Lambaréné. It was the worst moment in the year for the voyage, but Schweitzer took advantage of his inactivity on shipboard to complete his *Mysticism of Paul the Apostle* which he had been unable to finish in Europe.

His third visit to Lambaréné lasted two years. Not only did he redouble his work at the hospital, but he wrote his autobiography, which was published in both German and English in 1931 and is a mine of invaluable information. He also, at the request of those who had heard him speak in Europe, resumed the practice of preaching on Sundays, and thanks to his skilled interpreters he was able to touch the hearts of his African listeners. His language was as fervent as ever, and as quiet; and he kept his sermons, as he himself has said, "as concrete as possible". "Elementary experience" was their invariable base.

The days were as full as ever. Often they were extremely exhausting, and there was never any relief from the continual heat. Yet there was profound satisfaction in the work. It was during this sojourn that the Doctor heard of his election to an honorary doctorate at

Edinburgh. In February 1932 he decided to come to
Europe for a few months. During the voyage he worked
mainly on the address which he was to give, as holder
of the Goethe Prize, at Frankfurt on 22nd March 1932,
the centenary of the poet's death. He had thought of
declining this honour; but, having accepted it, he was
determined as always to make something exceptional
of his address. All those who heard him speak on that
day have an imperishable memory of it. Sandwiched
between the funeral march from the Eroica Symphony
and a Bach suite, Schweitzer began by speaking of
Goethe and the bases of his enduring greatness. He
then plunged his hearers into the anguished centre of
contemporary life with a comparison between the tragedy of Faust and the tragedy of the modern world and
its compulsive, demoniacal violence. He implored his
listeners to retain possession of their individual souls
and to be "men of contemplation—and yet men of action
also". It was one of his last visits to Weimar Germany;
he always refused to enter the "totalitarian state", and
his next visit to his friends in Frankfurt was to be
delayed for many years—years during which he was to
witness, as he had always apprehended, the hideous
facts of civil strife and world-wide war.

In 1932 he visited Holland, England, and Switzerland.
Whenever he could pause for a few days in Strasbourg,
and above all at Günsbach, visitors came pouring in,
though there was ever more and more work to be done.
He had already begun a new book. Originally it was
meant to be only one section of his vast survey of the
great religions of the world: a general review, in fact,
of Indian and Asian thought. On 15th March 1933 he
left for Lambaréné. He only stayed there until January

1934, when he returned to Europe for a lengthy lecture-tour. But while he was at Lambaréné there were new huts to be built, older ones to be re-arranged, and a host of medical points to be checked. Once back in Europe, his lectures—and especially the series to which he was committed in Oxford and Edinburgh—took up much of his time. In November 1934 he received his honorary doctorate at Edinburgh University; Pablo Casals was among his fellow-Doctors, and these two great servants of Bach are old and firm friends.

He finished his book *Indian Thought and its Development*, and it was at Strasbourg, on 14th January 1935, that he spent his sixtieth birthday. His friends—I can see it as if it were yesterday—came to bring him their good wishes, and on the table in the Rue des Greniers the heap of letters and telegrams grew higher and higher. Columbia Records had asked him to record a whole series of works by Bach, and he made these in Strasbourg itself, at the church of Ste Aurélie; the organ there was one of Silbermann's, which Schweitzer knew well and had re-modelled a few years earlier. He left for Africa in February 1935 and returned in August of the same year: his series of lectures of Edinburgh was still not completed. During the long lecture- and con-cert-tour which followed he worked on the proofs of *Indian Thought and its Development* and gave a great part of his time to the hospital: there were new doctors to be appointed, and new nurses; medical supplies to be dispatched in ever larger quantities, and contacts with medical colleagues to be strengthened and developed.

In February 1937 he left for his sixth visit to Lam-baréné. Once more we saw him off, in the station at Strasbourg, on the night-train that travelled direct to

Bordeaux; once again he smiled to us from the window of his compartment. But we knew how distressed he was by the rising temperature of the European political scene, and how it grieved him to watch the approach of all that he dreaded most. He couldn't come back in 1938, but he promised to come in the following year. In particular, he promised the organisers of the Strasbourg Festival, in which I was taking an active part, to do his best to contribute to the 1939 Festival; this was to be devoted entirely to Bach, and we had named him as its Honorary President.

Sure enough, on 12th January 1939 he sailed for Europe. On 5th February he was in Strasbourg; but he had no sooner settled into the Rue des Greniers than he decided to return to Africa. He had seen enough of Europe to realise that war was imminent; and his infallible instinct told him where his duty lay. He left for Bordeaux, sailed for Africa on the boat that had brought him to Europe, and was back in Lambaréné at the beginning of March. There was pain and grief in the messages that explained why he had left so abruptly. He did all that could be done to ensure that the work of the hospital would continue, no matter what happened in Europe, and that the organisation which had been built up in Lambaréné would not be dismantled a second time.

This sojourn, his seventh, lasted nearly ten years— till October 1948. War broke out and, as a result of the Gaullists' intervention, French Equatorial Africa was soon involved in it. The news reached us by wireless, and filled us with distress and amazement, that Lambaréné was in the thick of the struggle. Luckily both sides respected the hospital, but there was a moment at which the Doctor ran short of supplies.

Gradually communications were restored, and Madame Schweitzer was able to rejoin her husband from Switzerland where he had installed her before the war began.

Meanwhile, American aid was forthcoming and the hospital once again began to function at full stretch. On 14th January 1945 Schweitzer's seventieth birthday was celebrated at Lambaréné. Those who had been with him in Strasbourg ten years earlier were longing to see him back in France; but months, and indeed years, were to pass before he once again set sail for Europe. Since December 1944 he had been getting news from liberated Alsace, but the new outbreak of fighting in the Rhineland was to prove a source of redoubled anguish. At noon on 7th May 1945 he learnt of the cease-fire in Europe; one of his white patients had picked up the news on the Léopoldville radio. He has described his feelings at that moment, so concisely, and yet so completely, that I cannot do better than copy out his own words:

". . . I couldn't afford to get up from my desk. There were urgent letters to be finished. And then I had to go down to the hospital, where the patients (those with heart trouble, among others) would be expecting me at two o'clock. During the afternoon we tolled the bell and announced that the war was over. Later, although I was very tired, I had to drag myself off to the plantation to see how the work was getting on.

"It was only in the evening that I could have a few moments' quiet and imagine the meaning of the cease-fire in Europe—and what it must mean to those millions of people who, for the first time in years, could sleep without fear of bombardment. There was a rustle in the palms in the darkness outside when I took down a volume of Lao-Tse from my shelves. And this is what

I read, on the subject of wars and victories, in the work of that great Chinese thinker of the sixth century B.C.

" 'Weapons are evil things and should be shunned by the noble spirit. The noble spirit will take them up only as a final resort, for he values calm and peace above all things.

" 'He does not rejoice in victory. He who rejoices at such times rejoices in the slaughter of human beings.

" 'When a victory is celebrated, the victor should comport himself as if he were at a funeral. A multitude of men have been killed, and they should be wept for, with tears of compassion. That is why the man who is on the winning side should comport himself as if he were at a funeral.' "

The restoration of peace did not bring about an immediate improvement in the victualling of Lambaréné, or in the provision of medical supplies. It was a long time before the hard work of many and the generosity of others put the hospital back on its old peace-time footing. There was increased aid from America; Doctor Joy and Mr Arnold were among the first to reach Lambaréné and to give effect to the great new wave of sympathy for Schweitzer and his work; they were also able to take back news of his condition and state of mind. New doctors and nurses came out to reinforce the loyal nucleus; the hospital was re-equipped and, in the summer of 1948, the Doctor was able to envisage a visit to Europe. At the end of October he was back amongst us.

I cannot describe with what joy he was welcomed by those who had waited so long. The road to Günsbach was soon crowded with pilgrims. They found the Doctor at seventy-three, as strong and as upright as ever. His hair had silvered over and his face was thinner, but his

eyes—if such a thing were possible—seemed even
keener than before. The whole of Alsace was bent on
fêting him. His native town, Kaysersberg, Colmar,
Strasbourg, his University, and representative bodies of
every kind vied with one another in their touching ex-
pressions of regard for this great son of Alsace. Schweitzer himself remained simpler than ever. The many
ceremonies and the obligatory journeys never prevented
him from working with his usual methodical regularity.
No matter how full the day had been, the lamp was lit
every evening in his window, and passers-by could see
his head bent over his desk. And then, for the first time,
he made for the United States, where he had long been
known and admired. Although he could not accept the
innumerable invitations to lecture which had flowed
across the Atlantic, he had decided to go to Aspen for
the Congress which had been convened on the occasion
of the bi-centenary of the birth of Goethe. Once more
his address had immense repercussions, alike in Europe
and in America. He was received everywhere with the
utmost respect and enthusiasm, and the generosity of
his American admirers made it possible for him to envisage a great expansion of his struggle against leprosy.
They enabled him, in fact, to create a veritable township, in which lepers could profit by the most recent of
medical advances.

On 24th October 1949 he sailed back to Lambaréné,
after having the delight of greeting his grandchildren,
the family of his daughter and her husband, M. Eckert,
a Zurich organ-builder.

And so he began his eighth sojourn at Lambaréné.
During the following two years there was to be—especially in France—a great increase in his fame: that fame to

which he himself is so perfectly indifferent. For his own part he went on working: the years had diminished none of his intellectual energy, none of the warmth of his heart, none of the strength of his hands. When he had returned to Günsbach in 1948, and sat once more at the organ which is his particular creation ("My Arab steed", he calls it) he found that his powers as an executant were still perfectly intact.

The Doctor and his gallant team of assistants, old and new, carried on with the work that he had begun nearly forty years earlier. Meanwhile his books, translated into twenty languages—German, English, French, Spanish, to start with, and then into every tongue from the Baltic to the Mediterranean, and from Japanese to Arabic and Hindu—his books brought light into many a waiting heart. And so it was, too, with the books that were devoted to him, and the magazine articles, and the news stories. Popularity of this sort is the primary, the almost tangible manifestation of fame, and is like a wave that nothing can arrest. Confused and disordered as it may often be, there can be no stopping it. Schweitzer, the great solitary, was now hardly able to take up his knife and fork without its being the subject of a radio announcement. His birthdays were the occasion of world-wide celebration. In 1950 Gilbert Cesbron's play *Il est Minuit, Docteur Schweitzer*, was first produced—in Alsace, to begin with—and met with general enthusiasm. Despite all the precautions that were taken to conceal the date of his arrival in France, a mob of journalists was waiting at Bordeaux on 8th June 1951; and they photographed and interviewed Dr Schweitzer on the quayside where he had so often passed unperceived. The more enterprising among them even put to sea with the pilot in order to steal a march on their colleagues. The Doctor was at once irritated and amused by their assiduity, but his good nature led him to give in to their importunities. When finally he got free of them and went to the train he carried his own luggage and went to a third-class compartment. The train drew out in the limpid summer evening and bore him off to the well-loved landscape of Günsbach.

Madame Schweitzer had come to meet him at Bordeaux. At Günsbach Madame Martin was ready for him, in the office where more and more letters were piling up every day. Schweitzer had less than six months to spend in Europe, and, in addition to the tasks which he had set himself, there were innumerable visitors and delegations, each with a claim upon his time. At Frankfurt he was given the Peace Prize—and at once gave it back to the donors, with the request that it should be given to needy students. In Paris he saw one or two dear friends, among them Philipp the pianist, who was on holiday from America. And at Strasbourg he heard the last concerts of the 1951 Festival. I was lucky enough to hear them with him, after staying at Günsbach. After the Fifth Symphony of Jean Rivier— which he greatly liked—had been conducted by Ernest Bour, he heard Charles Münch conduct Honegger's Fifth Symphony. He was deeply affected by this splendid work, and insisted on seeing Honegger, who had long been one of his firmest admirers. I shall never forget the radiant smile with which Honegger received what was, for him, the supreme accolade—the approval of Albert Schweitzer. I was also much interested to be present when Queen Elisabeth of the Belgians came to Günsbach, on the first of several visits. After she had

E

left, the Doctor commented to me, "It's lucky that she is a Queen. She's a queen among women."

Shortly before he left once more for Africa, the Doctor was invited by the French Academy to fill the vacancy in its ranks left by the death of Marshal Pétain. He felt bound to accept this high honour; but in his letter of thanks he asked to be excused the traditional round of visits, and to be forgiven for his absence on the day of his election. For his cabin was already booked on the *Foucauld*, which was leaving on 23rd November, and on the day of his admission to the Académie de France the *Foucauld* put in at Conakry, where he gave an organ recital on behalf of the charities run by his old friend the Bishop of Conakry.

Many efforts had been made to keep him longer in Europe: to complete the ethical treatise on which he has been working for so many years; to settle the problems involved in the French translation of his works of philosophy and exegesis; and to round off, with his disciple Nies-Berger the edition of Bach's Chorale Preludes, which he had taken up after a lapse of many years. But he had made up his mind, and he kept to his decision, while yielding to his many supplicants to the extent of promising to return in the summer of 1952.

In that year the secret of his arrival was betrayed once again. Even the radio announced that he would be at Bordeaux on 28th July. As I write, the tireless exponent of goodwill-in-action is back at Günsbach, as we hope he will be often again. He has as usual innumerable things to do, a mass of visitors to meet, known and unknown, individuals and groups, and new organ-recordings to be prepared. Günsbach is already a place of pilgrimage. He plans to make rapid visits to certain countries—partly because of his own affection for them, partly because of their manifold services to Lambaréné. Time is too short for there to be any question of either concerts or lectures, apart from his postponed address to the French Academy. Then he will be off again on his way to Africa. And many of us will feel bereft of a father—gladly as we bow to the determination, the good sense and the abounding vigour of the man who heals souls as easily as bodies: the man who, for nearly sixty years, has given his whole life to the fight against evil and suffering; the man who, beneath the banner of spiritual liberty, has been the impassioned servant of all that is lovely and of good report.

Part II

HIS WORK

V. THE WISDOM OF ALBERT SCHWEIT-
ZER. THE PHILOSOPHER AND THE
THEOLOGIAN.

It would be impossible to give even the most summary
account of Albert Schweitzer's philosophical views in a
dozen pages. Yet neither his life, nor his work, nor he
himself can be understood without some knowledge of
his moral and spiritual position. It is for this reason
that those who know him only as a man of action, as a
combined doctor-and-apostle, or as an inspired organist,
must necessarily have far too simplified an image of
him.

Schweitzer, knowing that all philosophical "systems"
involve a certain artifice, has never aimed to create one.
So-called "pure speculation" has no charms for him; he
finds it pointless, where not actively harmful. His mind
inclines rather to history and the study of morals; he
has, in fact, put history to work in the service of morals;
and he has himself served morals not only in thought,
but in deed. One day he said to me "Whatever may have
come of Lambaréné, and whatever its place may have
been in my own life, it is primarily a *moral* experiment.
And that is how it should be thought of." Paul Bourget
ends his *Démon du Midi* with the often-quoted phrase
"We must make our lives fit our thoughts—or we shall
end by making our thoughts fit our lives." Schweitzer
had decided to make his life fit his thoughts, and he
brought off something that might have seemed im-

possible: having accepted certain laws of thought and belief, he put himself, body and soul, at the service of those laws, and has never ceased to observe them. His immense capacity for work, and the exceptional range of his interests, have both been determining factors. He has been, for instance, a great servant of music; yet the material rewards of his recitals and recordings have invariably been made over to the hospital which he had built with his own hands.

His life has been one long benefaction: thought and deed have been as one, and every increase in knowledge has been somewhere reflected in action. It was therefore natural that Schweitzer should break away from the formalism in which so many "professional" philosophers have been content to remain stuck; the obscurity of their language cannot conceal from us the Byzantine futility of their speculations. Knowing that the world cannot be explained in such terms, he has turned back to life, relying on the experiments of the past and on the experiments which he has himself conducted. Ever since 1899, he has told me, he has sought for a way of salvation. Animated by the desire to serve others and the will to do good, he has pressed on with his researches in the face of the rapid and melancholy decline of our civilisation. Only a coherent ethical system can provide the answer. Rationalism alone is a narrow creed, and one that is quickly exhausted; there is, on the other hand, illimitable power in a conviction that goes beyond reason. Illimitable, too, is the will-to-life which springs from such convictions. It is only by an ethical mysticism that we can recapture the true sense of life and rediscover how to think in religious terms.

This is how Schweitzer, a Christian by heredity and

vocation alike, was led to proclaim the principle of reverence-for-life, a phrase which in the original German, *Ehrfurcht vor dem Leben*, has a nuance of fear which is lacking from its English equivalent. This principle is the centre and keystone of his morality, and every one of his books is built round it. His work began with an immense amount of preliminary historical research and comparative study. In his *Philosophy of Civilisation* he starts from the Greek and Roman philosophers, turns to the Renaissance and the post-Renaissance, examines Kant, Spinoza, Leibnitz, Fichte, Goethe, Hegel, and winds up with Schopenhauer and Nietzsche. After this enormous survey he is ready to examine the problem of ethics in the light of the history of ethics, and thence to establish his personal position. For is it not the case that all philosophies lead to one of two contradictory positions? Either they turn to face life and the world, or they deny their existence.

Schweitzer has no time for the latter view. He finally reaches a new and positive outlook. "All that fosters and encourages life is Good; and all that destroys and mutilates it is Evil." In saying this, of course, he goes straight back to the religion of Jesus. And he has a striking image for the relation of ethics to mysticism. "Mysticism is not the flower, but the stalk. Ethics is the flower." If the world remains an impenetrable mystery, the mystical ethic of Schweitzer allows him, none the less, to face and resolve the problem which he considers fundamental: man's relations not only with other men, but with all other living things, and therefore with the universe.

In doing this, the mature thinker joins hands with the infant Schweitzer—the little Alsatian boy who, praying with his mother before going to sleep, added to his prayers these Franciscan phrases in which his intuition led him straight to the heart of the matter: "O good Lord, protect and bless all things that breathe, preserve all living things from evil and suffer them to sleep in peace . . ." Thence, too, comes Schweitzer's detestation of all unnecessary suffering: by this he means, among other things, those abominable pastimes which involve the wounding or killing of animals. Hunting and fishing he abhors, when they are practised as "pleasures". Likewise the abuse of vivisection; and the pointless destruction of plants and trees. On all these things, the Doctor has repeatedly made his point of view clear. Nor can the fact be stated too often: there are many so-called admirers and followers of Schweitzer who fail to realise how often they practise those things which most excite his wrath.

Meanwhile our materialistic "civilisation" (as we still call it) continues to produce results which are not merely disappointing, but positively tragic. And there too we have only to open our hearts to Schweitzer and face the facts: the Hegelian notion of Progress, like the utopias proffered by the demagogues, has already gone by the board. We must face the truth that this degeneration is the reflection of a *spiritual* decline. That is why our clamorous appeals to "law" and "justice" lead only to the violation of the very things which have been invoked; that is why the blind forces of the universe, which have been conjured up for our destruction, have inaugurated an era of violence, cruelty and unprecedented destruction. How Mephistopheles must laugh! Schweitzer saw it all coming: already in 1922 he foretold that things would go from bad to worse, and History

has proved him all too correct. Rabelais too, in spite of
his jester's costume, could read the future. "Irrespon-
sible knowledge", he said, "means the downfall of the
soul." A civilisation which lives by appearances and has
cast aside the only law that matters, the moral law, is
bound for disaster. When the life of the spirit no longer
takes precedence over the discoveries of science, catas-
trophe cannot be long in coming. Schweitzer's fore-
bodings have become reality; the weapons of destruction have reached the proportions of nightmare.
Can they still be kept in check?

Yes, they can. But only if mankind, in its despair and
its anguish, can recover its sense of spiritual liberty:
if it can rescue that liberty from the blind masses, and
from the leaders whom those masses have found within
their own ranks: if it can rediscover the laws of reverence-for-life and of abounding love-in-action. Such is
Schweitzer's conclusion, and he never tires of asserting
it. He counters the deadly pessimism of the intellectuals
with the will to love and the will to believe. His appeal
is to the necessity of belief in the spirit, in love, in
loving-kindness and the instincts of peace. It is not
surprising that such a doctrine should find an increas-
ingly responsive audience in every part of the world.
The Doctor's message has been translated into innumerable languages, and in every one of them it has
been welcomed as a blessing. Men and women everywhere have recognised in it the clear and cogent expression of ideas which they themselves had been
nourishing, confusedly, in their hearts. Schweitzer's last
word on the subject is a masterly summing-up: "The

notion of love is a ray of spiritual light which shines
upon us from an infinite distance. The man whose life is

charity will come to live in God and with God; so doing, he will possess the only thing that really matters."

In the second volume of his unfinished *Philosophy of Civilisation*, entitled *Civilisation and Ethics*, the ethics the Doctor proposes are those of the Kingdom of Heaven. In this book an ardent liberalism combats not only the excesses of rationalism but the abuses of the dogmatists. We can judge the sense and the general bearing of the book from these admirable phrases: "Just as a star is compelled by the brilliance within itself to shine out over the darkened world (even if there is no hope that it heralds a new dawn), so must the Christian blaze abroad the bright light of the Kingdom of God . . . We must never lose sight of one inexorable law: that we can only spread the Kingdom of God in the measure in which we carry it within us."

Indian Thought and its Development is, in Schweitzer's own words, a study in comparative philosophy. It is a sequel to the surveys which make up his *Philosophy of Civilisation*. The Doctor explains in his preface that as a young man he became interested in Indian philosophy while reading Schopenhauer. His interest proved to be lifelong; and there is a particular aptness in this, for Indian ethics stress not only man's relations with the rest of mankind, but his relations with all living creatures. Faithful to his invariable method of beginning with an historical survey and proceeding later to his own deductions and conclusions, Schweitzer starts with the origins of Brahman mysticism; studies Jainism; moves on to Buddha (stressing the fundamental differences which divide him from Jesus, despite certain similarities in the place allotted to charity in their ethical systems), and discusses the expansions and repercussions of Buddhism throughout Asia. Finally he takes us to modern times, by way of monotheistic Hinduism and the Bhagavad-Gita, and writes of Ramakrishna and Vivekânanda and of Gandhi and Tagore, with whom he was on terms of friendship. In his concluding chapter he reverts, with his usual cogency, to the doctrine of reverence-for-life and the necessity of "limitless ethics". One definition of this is especially clear and complete: "ethics is the acknowledgment of our responsibility towards all living things."

To cast an eye over Schweitzer's publications as a theologian and exegetist is to ponder once more the profound unity of his thought and his unvarying desire to serve his fellow-men. All these books were written between 1900 and 1913—before he went to Lambaréné, that is to say, and before he wrote any of his philosophical books. There are five of them: *The Mystery of the Kingdom of God*, *The Quest of the Historical Jesus* (of which an earlier, shorter version had appeared in 1906 under the title "From Reimarus to Wrede: a history of research into the Life of Jesus"); the *Psychiatric Study of Jesus* (his medical thesis, 1911); *Paul and his Interpreters*; and *The Mysticism of Paul the Apostle*. This last was published only in 1931, but Schweitzer wishes us to remember that all the preliminary work had been done before 1913.

The books total in all some 1,600 pages. When we remember that they were written during the years 1900–12, when Schweitzer was immensely active in many other fields, we must acknowledge a really formidable effort; both meditation and composition were on an heroic scale. Schweitzer has, of course, unusual powers of intuition and synthesis; but the research alone, and the preliminary studies, represent an astounding amount of work for a young man who was simultaneously making his way in several quite different fields. His contribution to theology and to exegesis is, moreover, as original and as important as ever, even though he has been too busy elsewhere to follow it up.

Schweitzer's works in this field centre, as we have seen, round the thought and person of Jesus on the one hand, and of St Paul on the other. They cannot, of course, be summarised in a few pages; but I should like to make the following observations, which are based upon notes made after conversations with Schweitzer.

Schweitzer's object has been to continue the work of his predecessors; even where he differs from the great historians of the past, he acknowledges their greatness. In particular he has followed the lines laid down by the great Strasbourg theologian Edmond Reuss. In *The Quest of the Historical Jesus* he surveyed all the lives of Jesus which had been published hitherto, first summarising their views, and then drawing his own conclusions as to the exact nature of the problem of the historical Jesus. Comparison and collation allowed him to prove the complete authenticity of the accounts of Jesus' public life which we read in the Gospels of the senior evangelists, Matthew and Mark. The historical reality of Jesus is now beyond question. Jesus went to Jerusalem in order that his trial, condemnation, and death might bring the Kingdom of Heaven on earth. In his detailed study of the trial of Jesus, Schweitzer has raised a fundamental problem: "Why did Jesus not consent to be stoned, as St Stephen had been? It was within the power of the Jewish ecclesiastical authorities to order this. And why did they bring him before Pilate, and so cause him to be crucified, according to the Roman method?"

Schweitzer gives the following explanation. The Sanhedrin considered that it was not for him, or for his authorities, to have Jesus arrested, tried, and stoned to death. Jesus had arrived in Jerusalem at the head of a great body of Galileans. These would not have tolerated a brutal intervention on the part of the Jewish authorities. What did the Jewish authorities decide? To arrest Jesus by night, to condemn him forthwith, and to ask Pilate to confirm their judgment at the earliest moment on the following morning. Jesus could then be crucified at once; and when the faithful gathered in the morning at the Temple and waited for Jesus to continue the struggle against the Sanhedrin, Jesus was already on the Cross.

Schweitzer also points out that in the Gospels of St Matthew and St Mark, Jesus does not present himself to the people as the Messiah. He keeps that fact a secret. He considers himself as the One who will be revealed in his Messianic glory at the coming of the Kingdom of God. When the crowd asked the Galileans who Jesus could be (at the time of his triumphal entry into Jerusalem) the answer was "It is Jesus, the prophet from Nazareth." And when Pilate and the high priest asked whether or not he considered himself as the Messiah, he replied "I am: and ye shall see the Son of Man sitting on the right hand of power, and coming in the clouds of heaven." ("Son of Man" is a synonym for Messiah, invented by the prophet Daniel.)

Schweitzer has also emphasised the sovereign character of Jesus' words and actions; "Every one of his sayings contains within it the 'total Jesus': whence their eternal and universal quality." If Jesus denies the world, his denial is quite different from that of the thinkers of India. If he rejects the ill-doing, suffering world, it is because he contrasts it with a perfected world, over which goodness and love will preside; the love which Jesus preaches is a positive, enthusiastic love, a love that leads to action.

Where St Paul is concerned, the prime result of Schweitzer's work is the conclusion that the mysticism of St Paul does not derive from that of his Greek predecessors. It has nothing to do with the Greek Mysteries, as we know them. It comes from the Judeo-Christian conception of the imminent arrival of the Kingdom of God. Paul recognised—and even to-day we can feel the scorching warmth of his affirmation—that in that Kingdom of God Christ was King. More clearly, in fact, than any other among Christ's disciples, he descried in Jesus the image of a belief that would be based upon ethics and upheld by love.

In St Paul's view, the world is already in transformation—and the faithful likewise; the natural state of man is being transformed into the supernatural condition of the Kingdom of God. The faithful are one in body and one in spirit with the resurrected Christ; they are, in fact, *in Christ*. It is this "being in Christ", this Judeo-Christian mysticism, which the Greeks, Justinius the Martyr and St Ignatius, have transposed into the Greek mystical conception of being "in Jesus by the spirit" (the *logos*). Man should renounce, therefore, his desire to know and to understand; he should give himself entirely to the only thing that matters, "the desire to be in God, to enjoy spiritual communion with Christ, and to raise himself above the mysteries which preoccupy him and the torment of insoluble problems."

Thus it is, at the climax of all his studies in philosophy, theology, and exegesis, that Schweitzer affirms
the continuity, and the profound unity, of his doctrine.
He does not linger over detail; with his powers of
intuition and synthesis, he dominates the problems
under discussion and keeps their general outline in view.
His warm heart irradiates that positive, illimitable love
which is based on reverence-for-life; and in all that he
does, reverence-for-life not only ensures for him a universal audience but makes of him, for all mankind, an
incomparably important human being, and one whose
goodness-in-action has no end.

IV. THE MUSICIAN AND THE ARTIST

Albert Schweitzer has served music in the same spirit
as he has composed his philosophical treatises and followed his vocation as a doctor. Once again we must
acclaim the unity of a life which accords perfectly with
the thought which has inspired it. From his earliest
youth, as indicated in the opening chapter of this book,
he displayed an extreme sensitivity to music. Music was
soon revealed to him for what it really is: not a mere
pastime, but a message of faith and of love. Let us pass
over the years of study and instruction and concentrate
on the threefold nature of Schweitzer's musical life.
Let us examine him as interpreter, as technician and
organ-builder, and as critic and historian.

He very soon became a great organist. What is almost miraculous is that he has remained one in spite
of the fact that for whole years together he is many
miles from the nearest organ and has only his pedal-
piano on which to practise. His passion for the organ
led him to take an interest in its construction, and
thenceforward to lead a veritable crusade on the technical aspects of the subject. And then, too, he has ap-
plied his historical and philosophical methods to the
study of musicology. It is this that gave novelty and
added importance to his *J. S. Bach* which, after half a
century, is as rich and original as ever. It is from this
book that our modern understanding of much of Bach's

work has stemmed; and it has opened many a new path
for Bach's interpreters.

It was in 1893 that Schweitzer first met Widor in
Paris. Despite the great difference in their ages they
became close friends (Widor, who was of Alsatian and
Hungarian extraction, was born in 1845, thirty years
earlier than Schweitzer). Since 1869 Widor has been
the official organist at St Sulpice, and the list of his
compositions—many of which, and especially his sym-
phonic works, have been unjustly forgotten—was already a long one. When he discussed Bach with Widor,
the young Schweitzer was able to draw upon his knowledge of theology and in this way to rediscover the
significance of Bach's setting. Before long his Bach
studies were taking on a quite unexpected amplitude.
Himself a great organist, Widor was deeply impressed
by Schweitzer's way of playing. Continual practice
made this steadily more and more remarkable. The
lessons of Marie Jaëll, that woman of genius, and of
Isidore Philipp, with whom Schweitzer is still on affectionate terms, contributed greatly to Schweitzer's form-
ation as an organist. He has often acknowledged
what he owes to his various teachers; but he would,
in any event, have become a master of the instrument by virtue of his exceptional spirituality; it is
this, after all, which brings him into such close spiritual harmony with the great musicians whom he serves
with such humble ardour. When Schweitzer mounts to
the organ-loft, he begins with a period of silent con-
centration. His friends know and respect this habit of
his. It begins on the way to the church; and when he is
actually seated before the organ he falls into an attitude
of prayerful quiet. He takes a long time to prepare each

piece; there, as in everything else, he likes to abolish the element of indecision completely. I remember the admirable metaphor which he once used in conversation: "Fine organ-playing," he said, "should be like a well-made rice-dish. Each grain should be firm and separate, no matter in what way the dish is prepared. Otherwise it turns into gruel." Schweitzer has been for many years a friend of Casals, Cortot, and Enesco; and, like these great and authentic human beings, he respects the composer's markings. Individual caprices have no meaning for him; nor has that infatuation with mere speed which marks the work of so many would-be virtuosi of our time. Their steeple-chasing methods obscure the real truth: that music is above all else the language of the heart, the language that is defeated by the prison-bars of grammar and syntax.

Albert Schweitzer soon became famous as an organist. In Paris he was the organist of the Bach Society, which his friend Gustave Bret had created and kept in being with such infectious enthusiasm. The proceeds from his recitals have often been a very important part of the moneys which he has been able to turn to charitable account. At the end of the 1914–18 war Schweitzer was delighted to find, in his own words, that he was "still an artist"(!); and he began to give concerts again. In 1936 a Society was formed with the object of persuading him to record a series of works by Bach. Sixteen years later, in September 1952, Schweitzer was once again to record the works of the great Cantor. As I was lucky enough to be present at the recording sessions both in 1936 and in 1952, I can speak with authority of what happened at those times. In 1936 the work was done in the church of Ste Aurélie in Strasbourg, where

Schweitzer had personally supervised the reconstruction of the Silbermann organ. The technical equipment was provided by a team of English specialists. The Doctor had prepared his interpretations with his usual minuteness, and when the trial discs were run through it was difficult to know which to prefer. In 1952 the records were made for an American firm. After reviewing many organs in his mind the Doctor decided to remain faithful to his nearest instrument, the organ in Günsbach itself. He loves this organ and has often praised it for its elasticity. "My Arab steed", he calls it. The few spectators at these later sessions were struck by the advances which had been made in the technique of recording. The Americans had sent over an immense lorry, most wonderfully equipped, which in itself constituted a complete recording factory. In the church itself there were two microphones. One was for communication with the lorry, the other for the actual recording. There were also two loud-speakers. The one transmitted messages from the lorry, the other played back the records themselves as soon as they were ready. Thus the Doctor could at once estimate the degree of his success; and, if he were not satisfied, he could re-record all or part of the work in question. Schweitzer played for weeks on end, and the recordings are worthy of his inspired and tireless execution.

We must also note the edition of Bach's organ works, which Schweitzer issued in collaboration with Widor. This began to appear in New York in 1911. It has never been finished, but thanks to the organist Nies Berger, who was born in Alsace and very often returns there from New York, the Doctor has decided to take it up again. With Nies Berger's help, he will complete this vast undertaking which includes not only the music itself, but extensive notes on the registration to be employed.

Schweitzer has explained that his passion for the organ is hereditary. Like his grandfather Schillinger, he soon got to grips with the problems of organ-construction. His concert-tours made him acquainted with a wide variety of organs and in 1906 he summarised his experiences in his study of organ-building in France and Germany. This was at once an expository and a comparative study of the subject; and in an appendix he gave a detailed account of two Parisian organs he especially admired—César Franck's Cavaillé-Coll at Ste Clotilde, and Widor's own, at St Sulpice. Both of these he knew intimately.

In 1909, while still a medical student, he took part in the musical congress in Vienna and presented, in collaboration with Xavier Mathias, a practical study of modern organ-building. He also took a successful hand in rescuing many old organs from destruction. The years have never dimmed his passionate interest in the organ. Every visit to Europe brings new proofs of this.

But it is not only organ-building that has attracted his most practical attention in the field of musical execution. He has also published a detailed and cogent essay upon the use of the round bow in Bach's Partitas for solo violin. He proves in this that with the Italian violin, which is now accepted everywhere, polyphonic passages can only be played *forte*, whereas the round bow, with its greater resilience, can give the strings their true sonority. The tone is never forced, and the bow can be adjusted with the aid of a simple lever-mechanism. I have myself heard this demonstrated by M. Frey of Mulhouse and Professor Schroeder of Cassel, and very convincing it was. The battle will have been won on the day when the study of the round bow is accepted in every school of music. The programme of the 1951 Bach Festival in Strasbourg included an excellent translation of this essay by Schweitzer's old friend, Professor Robert Minder of the Sorbonne.

We have still to discuss Schweitzer the exegetist. He has, of course, written the standard work on *J. S. Bach.* Since it was first published in Paris in 1905 this book has made its way throughout the world. It testifies not only to Schweitzer's great powers of construction but also to the immensity of his knowledge. It begins with an introductory essay in which Schweitzer acknowledges his debt to Eugène Münch, the teacher at Mulhouse who first revealed to him the glories of Bach. And with the name of Eugène Münch he couples that of his brother Ernest, and of the choir of St Guillaume at Strasbourg, which is now directed by Fritz Münch, one of Ernest's sons. He underlines the fact that his book is a contribution to aesthetics rather than to history. The history of Bach had already been explored to its depths by Spitta and the musicologists of the *Bachgesellschaft.*

Widor's preface confirms that the historians' researches into Bach's history had left such a mountain of material that there was a real need for a general survey, based on aesthetic principles. This was the book which Schweitzer had the honour of writing. Beginning with an examination of Bach's Chorales, with particular attention to their texts, he went on to survey the symbolism of Bach the "musician-poet". It had taken 155 years, Widor concluded, for us to master the symbolism of Bach, and "to gaze in full daylight upon the unity of his art."

The book[1] is divided into five main parts. A study of sacred music in Germany before Bach's time; the life and character of Bach; a study of the work, its genesis and its realisation; the symbolism of Bach's musical language; and the interpretation of his works.

i. This first section is a magisterial study of the Chorale up to and including Bach's lifetime, and of the history of the Cantata and the Passions before Bach.

ii. Schweitzer here evokes, with his usual clarity and authority (though he was very young at the time of writing), the life, the family, and the character of Bach, with its dominating theme of piety. "For Bach, music is above all the most effective way of glorifying God." His sublimest works were born of this mystical outlook.

iii. Schweitzer devotes fourteen chapters to a complete survey of the works of Bach. The continual symbolism and the admirable descriptive art are points on which he lays especial stress.

iv. Part iii leads naturally to Part iv, whose three chapters are of the utmost importance and originality. For the Doctor takes advantage of his survey of Bach's symbolism to hoist the whole question on to the general plane. In this way he manages to show the unity of art, and to prove, therefore, that "art for art's sake can only be an abstraction; art is the transmission of associations of ideas" (a remark which relates him to Baudelaire's famous *Correspondences*). These considerations touch on

[1] The reference here is to the work which Schweitzer wrote in French, *J. S. Bach, le musicien-poète* (Paris, 1905). He re-wrote the book in German at considerably greater length, *J. S. Bach* (Leipzig, 1908). It was from the German edition that the English translation was made by Ernest Newman in 1911.

Schweitzer's ethics, as much as on his aesthetics. In the two other chapters of Part iv, the Doctor gives thematic illustration of his theories about the musical language of the Cantatas, and we are reminded that the whole book derives from his profound knowledge of the Chorales.

v. This final section is devoted to the interpretation of Bach's works. In the light of his own experience, Schweitzer offers opinions and technical suggestions of the utmost interest. But it is typical of him that he ends with a quotation from Gevaert to the effect that "only one thing is really indispensable—that people of sensibility should be stirred."

And so, there too, we rediscover the unity of Schweitzer's deepest thoughts and the identity, throughout his life, of action and aspiration. And we remember how, when he was a small boy at Günsbach, music came to him as a revelation of those aspects of life—evil and suffering—from which other experiences turned him aside. The vital link, the invariable explanation, in Schweitzer's story is that form of reverence-for-life which we call love. Schweitzer the musician has always dedicated himself to its service—no less so, in fact, than Schweitzer the philosopher, with whom we have touched upon already, and Schweitzer the doctor-apostle, to whom we now have to turn.

VII. THE MANIFOLD MISSION. DOCTOR, COLONIST AND APOSTLE.

Schweitzer had no sooner qualified as a doctor than he went to Paris and took a special course in tropical medicine. He did this, in his usual methodical way, in order to equip himself as quickly as possible for his African mission. But on the very day of his arrival in the equatorial forest, Reality was to prove the most authoritative of teachers; the moment the news got round that a doctor had come to live in the region, patients poured in to see him. His installation was still quite precarious, however, and his only helpers were Madame Schweitzer—ever more tireless in her exertions—and one native male-nurse. Doctor Schweitzer has described these first perilous days in *On the Edge of the Primeval Forest*.

Before long there were radical changes. His first consulting-room, a disused chicken-house, was replaced by hutments which he himself built and equipped. An operating-theatre came next. Huts were built for the first in-patients. The whole enterprise had been condemned in advance; but common sense was confounded and all difficulties overcome by Schweitzer's indomitable will, his faith, and his reverence-for-life. He well knew, when he first picked on this remote country, that he would find himself in virgin forest, with no doctor for 300 miles around, an appalling climate, and a native population that was riddled with disease. Sleeping sickness alone had just massacred village after village.

Almost from the first, thirty to forty patients presented themselves every day. There were, in all, some 2,000 in the first nine months. The Doctor coped with every emergency: each patient was made to follow the hospital rules; consultations were put on a systematic basis; each patient was given a numbered cardboard disc, by which his case could be followed up and his dossier examined at any time. Despite the initial flimsiness of his surgical equipment, he managed to carry out a number of successful operations, and these had a great effect upon the natives' attitude to him. Already they considered that anaesthetics first killed the patient, and then brought him back to life by a miracle; and now they found that invalids whom they had considered to be ill beyond hope of recovery were completely restored by the Doctor's magic. The enormous hernias, the gigantic tumours (those brought on by elephantiasis may weigh up to sixty or eighty pounds), all had lost their deadly power. They had christened the Doctor *goanga*, the fetishist, and events were proving them right. For the savage, there are only three possible causes of illness: magic, the intervention of evil spirits, or the presence of a mysterious worm that eats away the inside of the body.

After a year, the Doctor surveyed the categories of illness which he had had to treat. The most widespread were: sleeping-sickness, leprosy, elephantiasis, osteomyelitis, malaria, amoebic dysentery. He also had a great many ulcers to deal with. Some of these, usually the largest, were syphilitic in origin. The native name for this disease was *pian* (or *framboesia*—on account of the crushed-raspberrylike appearance of the sores). He also distinguished ulcers of other kinds, such as the phagedena or rodent ulcer. This resulted in huge, foul-smelling sores which began with the feet and then spread upwards.

Among the cases of madness which the Doctor examined, some were brought on by poisoning. There were also serious cases of nicotine poisoning. The natives love tobacco, which is brought over from America in leaf-form and is sometimes used as payment. The abuse of nicotine led to a number of complaints, among them ineradicable constipation. Cancer and appendicitis, on the other hand, are practically unknown at Lambaréné.

The Doctor and his assistants gave particular attention to intestinal complaints. Amoebic dysentery is highly infectious, and they soon had to organise an isolation ward on this account. He also struggled particularly hard against the many illnesses which had their origin in intestinal worms. But it is above all with leprosy that he has secured wonderful results, especially in recent years and with new drugs from Europe and America. For a long time the improvement was very small, but thanks to American generosity he has now established a veritable village in which his leper-patients are isolated and given the most up-to-date of remedies. The results are remarkable, especially with the younger patients.

We have already had occasion to mention the names of certain among his assistants, doctors and nurses alike, who have taken a particularly distinguished part in the hospital's work; and we have indicated the great expansion which has been made possible, both in the surrounding buildings and in the central unit. This latter now includes operating theatres, out-patients' wards, consulting rooms, a dentist's room, and a

maternity room for native patients. An average of about
250 in-patients can be taken; this number is more than
doubled by the fact that their families usually come with
them. Three doctors, seven European nurses, and a
number of native male-nurses are continually at work
in this township, which is completed by an orchard, a
kitchen-garden, and a plantation of palm-trees. The
whole has been won, piece by piece, from the jungle,
and must be constantly defended against it.

The hospital represents year after year after year
of unrelenting work in a climate of merciless heat and
humidity. But Schweitzer has often stressed that the
reward of all this more-than-human effort is primarily
ethical. Those who work there know for certain that
they have diminished human suffering, have been of
service to life, and have thrust evil a little farther away.
And Schweitzer describes to us, in words which we
must quote in full, the reactions of a hernia-patient who
suddenly found himself relieved of the growth which
had so long tormented him:

"Hardly had he recovered his senses when he glanced
about him in amazement and repeated over and over
again 'It's stopped hurting! It's stopped, I tell you!'
His black hand groped for mine and wouldn't let go.
And I began telling him, and his friends, that it was
Our Lord's wish that the doctor and his wife should
come out to the Ogowe. In Europe, I told them, there
were other white men who had made it possible for
us to come out and live among our patients. And then
they asked me what manner of people these were. Who
were they? Where did they live? How did they know
what the natives were suffering? The African sun
blazed down and lit up the darkened hut as it stood in

its grove of coffee-shrubs. And we all, black men and white men alike, knew that we were bringing to life Christ's words: all men are brothers."

Schweitzer's life and thought have always had the firmest of moral bases; and he has concerned himself with souls as much as with bodies. His ideas on the problems of colonisation are set forth in several of his books, and especially in *On the Edge of the Primeval Forest*. There is a phrase that illustrates his general outlook in the matter:

"Are we the masters of this countryside, and this people, simply to make use of them as producers of raw material for our industries? Or is it our responsibility to create for them a new social order in which they lead a better life? In my opinion we have no right to colonise if we lack the moral authority to influence our subject peoples for good."

With his shrewd sense of reality, the Doctor has tackled and mastered a wide variety of problems: economic (for years I have had on my shelves—to take only one example—Schweitzer's exhaustive study of the problem of the timber-tree Okumé), sociological, and domestic. Among other things, the Doctor has treated the problem of polygamy among the natives, and has not hesitated to sum up as follows: "If we have to change the existing laws and customs, let us do nothing that is not absolutely necessary." He regards the natives as an older brother regards the younger sons. He acknowledges, too, and forcibly reminds us all, that something is owing to the natives for all the excesses which were committed by the earlier colonists. He holds that only those who have themselves known pain and anguish are equipped to build up a universal fraternity whose members will go out to the colonies and undertake the work of reparation.

The events of the last few years have by no means fulfilled Schweitzer's hopes and wishes. He regrets that the white man should have forgone his rôle of older brother, and links this abrogation with the general world-wide tendency to "suppress what remains of a patriarchal system, and to substitute a non-patriarchal system which is difficult to define and still more difficult to bring about".

He is careful, however, to avoid premature conclusions. He knows that contemporaries can never judge fairly of events with which they are themselves concerned. But in spite of his deliberately guarded way of writing, we can sense both distress and disquiet. Too often has Schweitzer seen his own moral principles opposed by policies which have little but illusions behind them. He himself has kept his spirit intact: may others profit by his great example!

"I shall be silent as a carp", Schweitzer spontaneously promised the directors of the Paris Missionary Society, doubtful of his orthodoxy, before he left Europe. He kept his word. While the hospital remained on its original site, its personnel could avail themselves, in any case, of the services held at the near-by Mission church.

But when it was moved to its present location in 1924, the situation was quite different. The Mission was far distant. The Doctor therefore decided to hold a service every Sunday. He himself has described the special circumstances of these services. First there comes a hymn, played either by Schweitzer himself on a portable harmonium or on a gramophone record. Then the Doctor stands in front of one of the hutments in the centre of the hospital, and begins to preach. Two interpreters stand beside him and, as he goes along, each translates his sermon into a different tongue. In this way the listeners have plenty of time to digest what they hear. For the same reason, the sermon is short and simple. The Doctor takes great care to adapt himself to an audience which, in general, knows nothing of the Bible and has to have everything explained to it. With the primeval forest all round him, Schweitzer recaptures the timeless essence of the Gospels. Some of his sermons have been noted down: sober and rudimentary in their symbolism as they are, they reveal the perennial Schweitzer, the servant of love, the preacher of reverence-for-life, the harbinger of the Kingdom of Heaven. Like everything else that he does, they have the stamp of an exceptional human being.

In July 1916, in one of the essays which make up *On the Edge of the Primeval Forest*, the Doctor summarised his findings in the matter of Christianity and the primitive peoples after his first three years in Africa. The savage, he noted, was readily accessible to the elements of religion, on account of his taste for meditation. The historical side of Christianity might be quite outside his ken, but he was quite susceptible to its moral conceptions, and might find in them a source of deliverance. Naturally amoral, he can none the less attain to a lofty system of morals. But the Doctor already urged the necessity of prudence; and with his usual foresight he warned his readers that the war must inevitably diminish the whites' prestige and hinder the expansion of missionary work. "Christianity," he said, "has achieved certain results by virtue of its being a religion of love. But these are offset by the fact that it has not been strong enough to bring about peace among the nations which adhere to it. Moreover Christianity has associated itself, during the war, with a great many amoral activities. When we preach the Gospel in distant countries we should not attempt to deny these melancholy facts, or to excuse them. We have not fulfilled our civilising mission as we should have done: and now we must resume it in a profounder and more ethical spirit."

Many attempts have been made to "define" Albert Schweitzer, and it seems to me that Georges Marchal, in his study of Schweitzer the theologian, has summed up his position as well as any. Schweitzer, he says, "has become a legend in his lifetime. Combining the Olympian grandeur of a Goethe with the fresh and smiling quality of a St Francis of Assisi, he is outlined on our horizon as an indomitable witness of the Spirit."

This sentence lays stress on two characteristic aspects of Schweitzer. Like Goethe, as Marchal says, he is a man of great power, a sovereign. Behind the curve of a lofty forehead there lies, in each case, an indefatigable curiosity and a store of great thoughts. But with Goethe it is the intellect that dominates, and all that goes with it—although Schweitzer has emphasised that Goethe was also, at times, a man of sensibility. In Schweitzer, sensibility and the will to moral action lie uppermost. Both men were by nature enthusiasts, authoritarians, despots even. Both have tamed themselves and acquired self-mastery. In Schweitzer's case, a fantastic vitality has always been at the service of the Good, and not merely of the Beautiful. His bearing and carriage epitomise that Olympian quality which he has in common with Goethe, and which in this case is allied with an expression of radiant good-nature, indeed of tenderness.

When Schweitzer walks out of his house, strong and upright as ever in his suit of semi-medical semi-parsonical black, he holds out his hand as a reigning monarch puts forth his sceptre. For Schweitzer, who has spent nearly all his life in the company of the poorest and humblest of men, can walk with the great of this earth on a footing of perfect equality. He is a natural leader: and that is why, in all his innumerable activities, he has been able to build, and organise, and direct.

But when he bends over one of his patients, or steers an inoffensive insect out of harm's way, he is nearer to St Francis of Assisi. His face clouds over when he speaks of human suffering, and at such moments there is in his eyes, even more than in what he says, a power that cannot be resisted. I remember that when I got off the bus at Günsbach, after not seeing him for nine years, and didn't want to let him carry my luggage, his first words were "Have you forgotten that I'm not a person to argue with?" What *is* the point, after all, of arguing with someone who is invariably right?

And yet, in any controversy, or when ideas are being exchanged on some problem of philosophy or aesthetics or sociology, nobody is more stimulating than Schweitzer. Fifty years have passed since he first dazzled and delighted his students in the Strasbourg theological seminary, but he has lost nothing of the freshness of mind and temper which then distinguished him. His conversation is full of contrasts: smiles and flashes of lightning, anecdotes and flights of speculation. As he stoops over a flower by the wayside or chats with a

G

passing shepherd, his mind keeps company with Bach and Goethe or soars among the everlasting truths of ethics.

Schweitzer is an Alsatian and bears, through and through, the stamp of his native land. He is a man of the river and the vineyards, a Rhinelander midway between two races and two civilisations. But he has never given way to the headlong passions of politics. Nationalism has no meaning for him. Nobody is better qualified to speak, on this point, than Robert Minder, who is himself an Alsatian and an old and close friend of the Doctor. He has put the point once and for all: "We must remember," he says, "that one of the most striking of Schweitzer's traits is his fidelity to his friends." As a child, Schweitzer grew up with a double loyalty, to France and to Germany. Some people—they are to be pitied—cannot understand this attitude, which is that of a true "citizen of the world". Even in Alsace itself, where he is loved and revered, and his visits are marked by innumerable acts of affecting homage, even there he meets with the most obstinate incomprehension. Those Alsatians who cannot enter into his thoughts do not hesitate to misrepresent his intentions and call his whole conduct in question. It has been so since the beginning of time: there are certain dark souls to whom an excess of light is embarrassing and painful.

Here I want to turn aside for a moment. The Doctor's world-wide celebrity in recent years has given rise to a great many manifestations of one sort and another. Some have been moving and effective: others unhappy and misleading. "Popularity is the bargain basement of fame", and Schweitzer's friends have often been stunned and horrified by what has been written in the newspapers by journalists with nothing better to say. Happily the Doctor himself is too busy to wade through the flood of often ill-informed eulogy. Once or twice, however, I have witnessed his irritation when an article has caught his eye: "I'd sooner be unknown in my own country than have them write me up like a prize-fighter!"

For the real Schweitzer is something finer than any figure of legend: he is, as he has always been, touchingly modest and simple, the living image of his unblemished spirit. He also has the true robust Alsatian sense of humour, and has always excelled in that full-flavoured repartee which is the speciality of the vineyard-country. Lately I was with him at Kaysersberg, where the Mayor and the Curé had asked him to look at the organ. As might be supposed, the little church of his native town was full to overflowing; the older citizens wanted to renew his acquaintance, and their juniors were eager for their first sight of so legendary a figure. The Doctor had a friendly word for everyone. Eventually he made for the organ-loft, only to find that the ladder which leads to it was in very bad repair. Hardly any of the steps were intact. Both Mayor and Curé wanted Schweitzer to wait while they fetched a better one, but he refused to do so and scrambled quickly and surely to the top. "My dear Mr Mayor," he said, "it's only a month since I climbed my own roof and refitted the tiles." And when he had finished his inspection and made his way down again, he said "Your organ's in good shape. With quite a modest expenditure on repairs, you'll have a remarkable instrument on your hands." And suddenly the nearly-eighty-year-old Doctor had a twinkle in his eye. "But before you start spending money," he said, "you'd really better get a new ladder. You can't always be sure of getting an organist as young as I am, you know."

Every morning, whether at Günsbach or at Lambaréné, letters now arrive by the bagful, and each one testifies to the excited attention with which the outer world follows his activities. He cannot, of course, read them all—moving as it would be to do so. What is remarkable is the size and universality of the audience. This is something that Field-Marshals and Prime Ministers can command; more rarely, it is accorded to a great artist or a creative spirit in some other field; but in the Doctor's case it is addressed to a moralist, in whom thought and action are one. This was recognised in America in 1949. Bruno Walter then wrote to me, "Schweitzer's visit to the United States has been more important, and has had wider repercussions, than that of any other visitor for years and years." It is a matter for reflection that more has been written about him in Japanese than in French. Across the world, and regardless of differences of race, culture, and religious aspiration, Schweitzer has touched the hearts and minds of men alike by his message and by the way in which his life has been its perfect illustration. He has provided one and all with a living source of encouragement. This great man speaks the language of the heart, and there is none by whom he cannot be understood. By his reverence-for-life, his *veneratio vitae*, his *Ehrfurcht vor dem Leben*, he has shown us why we are alive, and why we have reason to hope.

Conclusion

It was at Bayreuth, on the eve of a performance of *Parsifal*, in the summer of 1952, that I received a telegram announcing the Doctor's arrival at Günsbach. "Waiting for you" it said, and added Schweitzer's kind remembrances to Wolfgang and Wieland Wagner. Two days later I recrossed the Rhine, followed the valley of Upper Alsace as far as Colmar, and completed my journey on the tiny Munster railway, with its wooden coaches and overflowing load of young people. It was a magnificent evening in early August, and as the shadows lengthened there came a cool breeze from the wooded heights of the Vosges. I felt as if it were only yesterday that I had left this unchanging landscape.

Night was falling as we got on to the Munster road. We dined with Madame Schweitzer and took coffee with Madame Martin in the room next the big office. We exchanged news of Paris, Strasbourg and Bayreuth. A troop of boy-scouts had come to pay their respects to the Doctor and pitched their tents in the orchard. The smell of earth and the smell of the fields had been heightened all day by an implacable sun; and now it lay heavy all around us. The Doctor sketched out his plans: ". . . till November." "What—d'you mean you're not going to winter in Europe?" "They need me at Lambaréné." "Yes, but we need you here, too." He made no reply. His mind was already made up. He is as erect as ever, if not more so. He looks even better than he did last year. It seems incredible that he is approaching eighty years of age.

The organ came first: recording was due to begin in three weeks. The edition of Bach's Chorale Preludes had to be completed if possible: Nies Berger was over again from New York for the purpose. The address to the Académie to be written. There were essential journeys: to Frankfurt, above all, for the Goethe anniversary. There were innumerable medical matters to be seen to; and, above everything, at least one book to be finished if there was time. On top of it all, hundreds and hundreds of visitors; some by appointment, others unannounced, and not always opportune. The Doctor gave a barely perceptible shrug of the huge shoulders that had never bowed before trouble. "At Lambaréné," he said, "they've just rung the evening bell." His mind and his heart are ever divided between his two countries: his native Alsace, and the little world he has created in the Gabon. But in his general outlook upon the world the two become as one, and he concentrates all his ardour, all his tenderness, upon the tasks ahead of him.

I spoke to him about this book. When he replied, it was with a warmth that rewarded me a hundred times over. "At least you'll get it all right" he said. An hour later, in the quiet of my room, I sketched out the first draft of my study, under the same roof as the Doctor. Downstairs he was working away as tirelessly as ever, covering page after page with his noble, unchanging script.

"How long are you going to go on working like this?" said his wife not long ago. "As long as I can draw breath," he replied in that deep, grave, resonant voice of his. What else could he have said, after all?

Let us pray that for many years to come that great heart will go on beating, and that great mind be spared to give out its message. His life has been consecrated to all that is good. With perfect serenity he can watch for the slow expansion, on our human horizon, of those eternal lights which he has not presumed to explain to us, but towards which he is our surest guide.

TWO ADDRESSES
BY ALBERT SCHWEITZER

Through the kindness of Dr Schweitzer two of his recent addresses are included in this book.

The first, 'Childhood Recollections of Old Colmar', which forms a valuable pendant to his *Memoirs of Childhood and Youth*, is the substantial part of his speech at a reception given in his honour by the municipality in the Hôtel de Ville at Colmar on 23rd February 1949.

The second is the complete text of his address before l'Académie des Sciences Morales et Politiques on his official installation as a member of the Academy at the Institut de France on 20th October 1952.

CHILDHOOD RECOLLECTIONS OF OLD COLMAR.

In October 1893, when I paid my first visit to Paris, the whole city was *en fête*. A detachment of Russian sailors, under Admiral Avellan, was visiting Paris, and there were Franco-Russian celebrations everywhere. There were parades, and a torchlight procession in which the Russian sailors in their white uniforms stood out against the darkness of the crowd.

People were surprised that the "young man from the provinces" was not more impressed by it all. But these magical scenes had none of the brilliance, as I saw it, of the Colmar procession. *That* was what I really remembered. It was at Colmar that I first met with the great world. What happened in Paris was merely a second edition.

Nor was the Louvre, in my eyes, a rival to the Colmar Museum. It was to Colmar that I was bound by the luminous memories of childhood. It was there, after all, that I had seen the work of Maître Mathis, Grünewald as he was called.

I knew the Colmar Museum pretty well. At that time it was customary for the families of Colmar to give their visitors a good luncheon and take them to see the Museum. (It was usually on Thursdays that these visitors came in from the surrounding countryside.) I hope that, in spite of the cinemas and the sporting events, this tradition is still alive—and that, for the sake of its cultural value, as people now call it, it will continue.

When I used to visit the Museum with my godparents and their guests, we always began with the older masters. It was a matter of duty to show them our respect. If there was one among them who stood out, it was not Maître Mathis, but Schongauer. Grüne-wald's pictures were hung in a corner and wretchedly lit. Far be it from me to suggest that I "discovered" them in my childhood. But they attracted me. When our troop of visitors moved on into another room, I often remained behind, in front of the Grünewalds; and even-tually they had to come and fetch me. What attracted me in him—as far as I can remember—was the bril-liance and unexpectedness of his colours, and also his realism. In the room where Jesus was born, for in-stance, there was a wooden tub for the baby's bath, just like the ones at Günsbach, and a chamber-pot within reach. And how realistic, too, were the devils' faces, and those of the fantastic animals in the Tempta-tion of St Anthony! There was always something new to be discovered.

But what fascinated me most of all, where realism was concerned, was the hair of the Apostle St John, as he bends down to the despairing figure of Mary beneath the Cross. I gazed and gazed at the tousled mop of straw-coloured hair. It had a particular message for me. My own hair was always very untidy. In the Apostle St John I had a companion in misfortune. I pitied him as much as I pitied myself. As a boy, he must have suffered as I did, when the maid-of-all-work brushed my hair every morning. She really hurt me, that maid. There was nothing she wouldn't do to make my hair lie flat. When she combed it, she certainly went to work. She had a yellow stick of brilliantine—"cos-

metic" it was called—which she rubbed into my scalp
to make the hair stick down. She made it as neat as
the figures in a balance-sheet: but all to no purpose.
An hour later there was nothing left of the parting,
and my hair had reverted to normal.

And the things she said, while she was doing it!
The insults! "There's a lot in the way your hair grows
. . . Unruly within, unruly without . . ." She was al-
ways inventing new things of that sort.

He too, I said to myself as I looked at St John—he
too has lived through this anguish of body and soul. I
found great consolation in my link with the Apostle.
For although I thought myself an obedient and disci-
plined young person, I was beginning to have doubts.
Could there be something in what the maid said? Could
my untidy hair have that dark significance? Did it
really foreshadow a lifetime of reprobation? I was
beginning to have a kind of inferiority complex. It was
Grünewald's St John who set me free. When I looked at
him, I argued with myself like this: St John's hair is
quite as untidy as yours, but it didn't prevent him from
being one of the Apostles. Therefore it can't be true
that you can read a man's character in his hair. And in
this way I began to free myself from the fears which had
taken hold of me, and were eating into me, and had
darkened the skies beneath which I was living.

Yet it was at Colmar, though not in the Museum,
that I became acquainted with Evil. It happened that I
became guilty by involuntary complicity, one of the
most complex of moral predicaments.

One Sunday afternoon my godmother Barth had to
go out. She left me with the two maids. (At that time
even the households of the *petite bourgeoisie* had two

maids.) I heard her say to these two maids, as she went out, that they should take me for a walk—but a short one—and that they were to keep a close watch upon all that I did. Hardly had she and her daughter left the house when the two maids and I set off on the road to Horbourg. Soon we heard a band playing. So it was the Horweriger Kilb, or Horbourg Fair, that attracted them! We were no sooner there than we found ourselves on the dance-floor and were swept up in the *contre-danse*. It was the real old *contre-danse*—something that you don't see any more—in which two lines of dancers, men and women, face one another. Their evolutions were not at all like the quadrille or the lancers, as we now know them. Back and forth they danced, and through and across. The two maids took excellent care of me. One took my right hand, the other my left. And each had, on her other side, a cavalier who interested her much more than I. For the whole of the afternoon I went forward, and I went back, and I pirouetted. And that was how I was initiated, at the Horweriger Kilb, into the secrets of the *contre-danse*.

As we scampered home, I came face to face with the problem of Guilt. "There's no need to say we've been at the fair," the maids insinuated. I was proud that they should trust me so far; but I was also disturbed. On the one hand I was on fire with chivalry. On the other, I should have to tell a lie, if I was to keep faith with these two sterling girls. Luckily, as happens at times to all of us, I was spared the ordeal. Neither they nor I had to stray from the truth. When my godmother came back, all she said was "Nice, was it?" And they replied: "Very nice, Madam." As to where we had been, and what we had done, nothing was said.

There was another case of guilt by involuntary complicity which didn't turn out so well. One afternoon my godmother entrusted me—I'm not quite sure why—to a boy from Colmar who was a little older than myself. His mother was a friend both of my godmother and of my mother. Though only slightly older than myself, he was a great deal more developed. "You'll look after him properly, won't you?" said my godmother. "You mustn't go to the Lauch, and above all you mustn't go boating." The older boy took note of these instructions, and we went out of the house, and along a great many narrow streets that I'd never been in before, and eventually we got out of the town. We found ourselves on the banks of the Lauch. I'd never seen a real river before, or real boats—not painted ones, but real ones that floated on the water, with great loads of vegetables on board and a man in the stern to steer them. It made the profoundest impression upon me. For, after having wanted to be a coachman, and later a pastry-cook, I had just decided to become a sailor. My mother was greatly distressed about this and had tried to deter me by pointing out how inconvenient it was to sleep in a hammock instead of a bed.

My companion turned to me and murmured, "Let's find one that's not properly tied up." He found one, untied it, jumped aboard and signed to me to get in too. "Remember what your mummy said!" I begged him. "Remember what my godmother said! We mustn't do it!" He didn't deign to reply, but looked at me as if I had fallen out of the moon and was speaking some unknown language. He didn't even try to find excuses for not obeying. He merely implied by his attitude that obedience, in his eyes, was a prejudice to be abandoned:

a notion so far beneath him that there was no point in acknowledging it. It was an attitude of mind that I had not imagined possible. When later, towards 1893, as an undergraduate, I read what Nietszche had written a few years before—it was beginning to make something of a stir—I found nothing surprising in his intention to go "beyond good and evil". There was nothing in Nietzsche that had not been revealed to me, without a word spoken, in that scene on the banks of the Lauch. And, for an instant, as I boarded the boat under the imperious gaze of my companion, I had been one with Nietszche.

It certainly was not the first time that that boy had been out in a boat. He knew just what to do. As we skimmed along beneath the trees, the busy stream was filled with craft laden to the water-line with vegetables.

For all my remorse at having yielded to temptation, I was thoroughly enjoying the trip. I was afloat at last! What I had long dreamed of had come true.

Then we heard voices in the distance, and I came back from dreamland. My companion listened carefully. His face grew dark. "Better be going back," he said.

I realised that something was wrong. We must have been betrayed. One of the boatmen must have recognised our vessel and given its owner the tip. When we got back, he was there, all right, and in a terrible rage. "I'll tell your mother this time," he said to my companion. And, sure enough, he did.

When my godmother took me home to Günsbach, and my mother asked, as usual, if I had been a good boy, she had to say—and I can hear her now—"Not altogether." When my mother asked her to explain what had happened, she did so, taking care to say that I had

been influenced by an older boy. Despite this extenuat-
ing circumstance, I was punished and had to do penance
as if the guilt had been all my own.

Still, guilty or not, I'd been out in a boat!

Yes, it was at Colmar that I set sail for the first time.
And it was at Colmar, too, that I first glimpsed the
grand object of all my travels. The Bruat monument,
with its statues, each representing some distant people,
had always fascinated me. I especially liked the statue
of the African negro. In the attitude and features of
this black giant there was a certain melancholy which
aroused my compassion and led me to reflect upon the
fate of the negroes. Whenever we went to the Champ
de Mars I asked if we could make the little detour
which would allow me to pause in front of the Bruat
monument.

Later, when I lived in Mulhouse and went to school
there, I still went to look at the statue whenever I was
in Colmar. After 1896, when my sister married M.
Jules Ehretsmann, who had a hat-shop in the Place de la
Cathédrale, I often stayed in Colmar. I came to know
the town and its inhabitants really well, and I particularly admired the incomparable carillon of St Martin's
church; but I remained faithful to my rendezvous with
the African negro. It was this statue of Bartholdi which
summoned me, at the age of thirty, to live and work in
Africa.

And in 1913, when for the first time I sailed down the
African seaboard, I discovered the race of giants from
among whom Bartholdi must have chosen his model.
They live along the Ivory Coast.

H

THE PROBLEM OF ETHICS IN THE EVO-
LUTION OF HUMAN THOUGHT.

In the space of a single lecture I can give only a very summary account of the problem of ethics in the evolution of human thought. I shall therefore confine myself to the broad outlines of that evolution, and in doing so shall attempt to make them as clear as possible.

What we call "ethics" and "morality", in terms borrowed respectively from Greek and Latin, may broadly be said to be concerned with the problem of how to behave well towards ourselves and towards others. We feel obliged to think, not only of our own well-being, but of that of other people, and of society in general.

The first stage in the development of ethics began with the idea that this "thinking of others" should be put on an ever-broader basis. Primitive man thinks of others only within the narrowest limits. He confines himself to those whom he sees as distantly related to himself by blood: the members of his tribe, that is to say, whom he regards as constituents of the same large family. I speak from experience in this. My patients at Lambaréné illustrate the point. Sometimes I ask a savage of that sort to render certain little services to a fellow-patient who cannot look after himself. He will at once ask whether the other man is a member of his tribe. And if the answer is "No", he will frankly reply: "This not brother for me." Neither persuasion nor threats will induce him to commit the unimaginable

114

action and put himself out for a stranger. It is I who have to give in.

But as men think more and more about themselves, and about their behaviour to others, they come to realise that other men, as such, are their kith and their kin. And slowly, with the evolution of ethics, they see the circle of their responsibilities grow wider and wider until it includes every human being with whom they have any sort of association.

It is on this level of understanding that we find the Chinese thinkers: Lao Tse, born in 604 B.C., Kung Tsu (Confucius), 551–479 B.C.; Meng Tsu, 372–289 B.C.; Chuang Tsu, in the fourth century B.C., and the Hebrew prophets Amos, Hosea, Isaiah in the eighth century B.C. The idea that we each of us have a responsibility towards every other human being was put forward by Jesus and St Paul and is an integral part of Christian ethics.

For the great thinkers of India, be they Brahmans, or Buddhists, or Hindus, the idea of the universal brotherhood of man is part of the metaphysical idea of existence. But it is not easy for them to incorporate it in their ethical systems—for the existence of castes, in India, has erected barriers between man and man which have been sanctified by tradition and cannot now be abolished.

Nor, in the seventh century B.C., could Zoroaster encompass the notion of the brotherhood of man. He had to distinguish between those who believed in Ormuzd, the god of goodness and light, and the unbelievers, who remained under the aegis of the demons. He insisted that the believers, in their struggle to bring about the reign of Ormuzd, should consider the unbelievers as their enemies and treat them accordingly. To understand the situation, we must remember that

H*

the believers were Bactrian tribesmen who had adopted a sedentary mode of life and wanted to live as honest and peaceable farmers; the unbelievers were tribes who had remained nomadic, lived in the desert, and supported themselves by pillage.

Plato, Aristotle, and the other thinkers of the classical period of Greek philosophy thought only in terms of the Greek—the Greek freeman, moreover, who was not concerned to earn his own living. Those who did not belong to that aristocracy they regarded as inferior beings and unworthy of serious attention. Only in the second period of Greek thought—that in which Stoicism and epicureanism flowered simultaneously—did both schools become willing to accept the idea of human equality, and of the intrinsic interest of human beings as such. The most remarkable champion of this new conception was the Stoic, Panaetius, who lived in the second century (180–110) B.C. It is Panaetius who is the prophet of humanism.

The idea of the brotherhood of man never became popular in ancient times. But there is great importance for the future in the fact that philosophers should have acclaimed it as eminently rational. We must admit, though, that the idea that a human being as such has a right to our interest has never enjoyed the full authority to which it might lay claim. Right up to our own time it has been menaced, as it is to-day, by the importance which we ascribe to differences of race, or religious belief, or nationality. It is these differences which make us look upon our kinsman as a stranger deserving of indifference, if not, indeed, of contempt.

Anyone who analyses the development of ethics must take into account the influence which is exerted upon

ethics by the particular conception of the world to which
it is related. There is, of course, a fundamental difference
between these various conceptions. This difference lies
in the particular way of looking upon the world itself.
Some thinkers believe that we should take an affirmative
view of the world—interest ourselves, that is to say, in
its affairs and in the part we ourselves play in them.
Others take a negative view, and advise us to take no
interest at all in the world, or in our own existence
within it. Of these two attitudes, the affirmative is
nearer to nature; the negative view does violence to it.
The one invites us to be at home in the world and to
take a vigorous part in its affairs; the other urges us to
live in it as strangers and to choose non-activity as the
basis of our life here. Ethics, as such, belongs to the
affirmative faction. It springs from the need to act; and
to act for good. Consequently the affirmation of the world
is favourable to the development of ethics; the negative
attitude, on the other hand, must thwart that development. In the first case ethics can offer itself for what it
is; in the second, it must give up the idea of doing so.

The thinkers of India deny the world. So do the
Christians of antiquity and of the Middle Ages; the
Chinese sages, the Hebrew prophets, Zoroaster, and
the European thinkers of the Renaissance and modern
times—all are champions of affirmation.

The Indian thinkers denied the world because they
were convinced that true existence is immaterial, im-
mutable, and eternal, and that the existence of the
material world is artificial, deceptive, and ephemeral.
The world which we like to consider real is merely, in
their eyes, a mirage of the immaterial world in time and
space. It is a mistake for us to interest ourselves in this

phantasmagoria and in the part we play in it. Non-activity is the only form of behaviour that is compatible with a knowledge of the true nature of existence. Of course non-activity has an ethical quality, in a certain degree. A man who renounces the things of this world renounces with them the egoism which material interests and vulgar covetousness would otherwise inspire in him. Moreover, non-activity implies non-violence. It saves a man from the danger of harming others by acts of violence.

Non-violence is extolled by the philosophers of Brahmanism, Sankhya, and Jainism. Like Buddha, they consider it the high-point of ethics. It is, however, imperfect and incomplete. It allows a man to be egoistic to the point of thinking of nothing but his own salvation. This he hopes to secure by a mode of life which conforms to a true knowledge of the nature of existence. It exacts this, not in the name of compassion, but in the name of a metaphysical theory; and though it asks him to abstain from evil it does not require him to act in accordance with the wish to do good.

Only an ethical system which is allied to the affirmation of the world can be natural and complete. If the Indian thinkers take it into their heads to yield to the promptings of an ethic more generous than that of *ahimsa*, they can do so only by making concessions to the affirmative point of view—and to the principle of activity. When Buddha takes a stand against the coldness of the Brahman doctrine and preaches the virtues of pity he can hardly resist the temptation to break free of the principle of non-activity. More than once he gives in to it and cannot help committing acts of charity or recommending his disciples to do the same. Under

the cover of ethics, the affirmation of the world carries
on an underground struggle, for century after century
in India, against the principle of non-activity. In the
Hindu religion, which is a religious reaction against
the exactions of Brahmanism, this affirmation actually
gets recognised as the equal of non-activity. The entente between them is proclaimed and specified in the
Bhagavad-Gita, a didactic poem which is incorporated
in the great epic of the Mahabharata.

The Bhagavad-Gita admits the Brahman conception
of the world. It recognises that the material world has
only a deceptive reality and cannot claim to engage our
interest. It is merely, the poem says, an amusing spectacle which God has mounted for his own diversion.
It is only as a spectator, therefore, that man is authorised
to take part in it. But he has the right to suppose that
he is to continue playing his part in the entertainment.
He is justified in doing so by the fact that he knows
why he is doing it. The man who goes about his work
in the world with no other intention than that of doing
God's will pursues the truth every bit as effectively
as he who opts for non-activity. Undiscerning activity, on
the other hand—activity which is prompted by interest in
the world and the wish to achieve some object, however
trivial—such activity is wrong and cannot be justified.

No ethic worthy of the name can be satisfied by the
concept of the world as a diversion which God has put
up for his amusement. True ethics asserts the necessity
of action. The theory did, however, allow ethics to keep
going in India at a time when its existence was threat-
ened by Brahmanism.

Contemporary thinkers in India make great concessions to the principle of activity, and affirm that it is

also to be found in the Upanishads. That is quite true.
The explanation is that in ancient times, as we learn
from the Veda hymns, the Aryans of India led a life
that was filled with a naïve delight in living. The
Brahman doctrine of the denial of the world only appears
alongside the doctrine of affirmation in the Upanishads
—sacred texts that date from the beginning of the first
millennium before Christ.

The Christianity of antiquity and the Middle Ages
preaches the denial of the world but does not, as a
consequence, enjoin non-activity. This peculiarity derives from the fact that its denial of the world is quite
different from that preached by the Indians. Christianity
declared that the world as we know it is not a phantasmagoria, but an imperfect world which is destined to
be transformed into the perfect world: that of the
Kingdom of God. The idea of the Kingdom of God was
created by the Hebrew prophets of the eighth century
B.C. It is also at the heart of the religion founded by
Zoroaster in the seventh century B.C.

Jesus announced the imminent transformation of the
material world into the world of the Kingdom of God.
He exhorted mankind to seek that perfection which
would enable them to enjoy a new existence in the new
world. He preached the abandonment of the things of
this world. To do good was the whole duty of man.
Man was allowed, in fact, to be indifferent to the world,
but not to his duty towards other men. Action keeps all its
rights, in the Christian ethic, and all its obligations too.
That is where it differs from the ethic of Buddha, with
which it has in common the idea of compassion. Animated as it is by the spirit of activity, Christian ethics

retains an affinity with the affirmation of the world.

The early Christians regarded the transformation of the world into the Kingdom of God as near at hand; but it has never occurred. Therefore during antiquity and the Middle Ages Christians despaired of this world and yet had none of those hopes which had buoyed up the early Christians. It would have been natural had they come round to the affirmation of the world. Their ethic of activity made it quite possible. But in antiquity and the Middle Ages there did not exist that passionate affirmation of the world which alone would have served the purpose. This passionate affirmation came into being at the time of the Renaissance. Christianity joined forces with it during the sixteenth and seventeenth centuries. Along with the ideal of self-perfection which it derived from Jesus, its ethics now embraced the Renaissance ideal: that of creating new and better conditions, material and spiritual alike, in which human beings could live together in society. Thenceforward Christian ethics had a specific end in view and could attain to their fullest development. The civilisation in which we live, and which we now have to sustain and to perfect, was born of the union between Christianity and the enthusiastic affirmation of the world which we owe to the Renaissance. The ethical conceptions of both Zoroaster and the Chinese sages were affiliated, from the very beginning, with the affirmation of the world. They, too, carry within themselves energies which could bring forth a civilisation based on ethics.

After attaining a certain level, ethics tend to develop in depth. This tendency manifests itself in the compulsive search for the fundamental principle of good.

Ethics no longer finds complete satisfaction in defining, enumerating, and enjoining various virtues and various duties. It seeks to analyse the link which unites them in their diversity, and to discover how it is that they all flow from a single conception of good. It was in this way that the great Chinese sages came to proclaim goodwill towards all fellow-men as the root of virtue. Even before Jesus, Hebrew ethics concerned itself with the problem of the one great Commandment: the law which was to comprise all law. In accord with the traditions of Hebrew theology, Jesus raised love to the rank of the supreme commandment.

In the first century of the Christian era certain Stoics followed the path laid down by Panaetius, the creator of the idea of humanism. They too came to consider love as the virtue of virtues. These men were Seneca, Epictetus, and the Emperor Marcus Aurelius. Fundamentally their ethic was that of the great Chinese sages. They had in common with them not only the principle of love, but—what is really important—the conviction that it stems from reason and is fundamentally reasonable.

During the first and second centuries of our era, Greco-Roman philosophy came, therefore, to profess the same ethical ideal as Christianity. There seemed every possibility of an entente between Christianity and the ancient world. Nothing came of it. The ethics of Stoicism never became popular. Moreover the Stoics considered Christianity as the worst of superstitions. Was it not based on a "divine revelation" that had occurred in the person of Jesus Christ? Did not Christians await the miraculous coming of a new world? Christianity, for its part, despised philosophy as mere

terrestrial wisdom. They were also divided by the fact
that philosophy kept to the idea of the affirmation of
the world, and the Christians to its denial. No agree-
ment was possible.

And yet, centuries later, they did reach an understanding. In the sixteenth and seventeenth centuries
Christianity became familiar with the passionate affirmation of the world which the Renaissance had bequeathed
to European thought. It also made the acquaintance of
the ethics of Stoicism, and was amazed to find that
Jesus' principle of love was there put forward as one
of the truths of reason. Among the thinkers who recognised their double allegiance—to Christianity and to
Stoicism—were Erasmus and Hugo Grotius.

Under the influence of Christianity, philosophical
ethics acquired an element of passion which they had
not previously possessed. Under the influence of philosophy, Christian ethics began to reflect upon what it
owed to itself and what it had to accomplish in the
world. Consequently there arose a spirit which would
no longer tolerate the injustice, the cruelty, and the
harmful superstitions which it had previously allowed.
Torture was abolished, and with it the scourge of
sorcery trials. Inhuman laws gave place to others more
clement. Reforms unprecedented in human history were
conceived and carried out in the first excitement of the
discovery that the principle of love is ordained by
reason.

Certain eighteenth-century philosophers — among
them Hartley, Baron d'Holbach, Helvétius and Bentham
—thought that the argument of sheer utility was sufficient to demonstrate the rational necessity of altruism.

The Chinese and the Stoics had also advanced this argument, but they had used others as well. The eighteenth-century thesis was that altruism is merely an enlightened form of egoism, and a conclusion drawn from the fact that the well-being of individuals, and of society as a whole, can only be assured by a system of mutual devotion. This superficial view was contested by Kant, among others, and by the Scottish philosopher David Hume. Kant, wishing to defend the dignity of ethics, went so far as to say that its utility should not be taken into consideration at all. Manifest as it may be, it should not, he said, be accepted as an ethical motive. The doctrine of the categorical imperative asserts that the commands of ethics are absolute. It is our conscience that reveals to us what is right and what is wrong, and we have only to obey. We carry within us a moral law which gives us the certainty of belonging not only to the world as we know it in time and space but also to the world as such—the world, that is to say, of the spirit.

Hume, on the other hand, proceeds empirically in his attack upon the utilitarian thesis. Analysing the motives of ethics, he concludes that it is sentiment, above all, which governs them. Nature, he argues, has endowed us with the faculty of sympathy, and it is this that allows us, and in fact compels us, to enter into the joys, the apprehensions, and the sufferings of others. We are, he says, like strings that vibrate in unison with those of the orchestra. It is this sympathy which leads us to devote ourselves to others and to wish to contribute to their well-being and to that of society. Philosophy since Hume—if we leave Nietzsche out of account—has never seriously questioned that ethic is above all a matter of compassion.

But where does this leave ethics? Can it limit and define our obligations towards our fellow-men? Can it reconcile egoism and altruism, as the utilitarian theory attempted to do?

Hume barely considers the question. Nor has any later philosopher felt bound to consider the consequences of the principle of devotion-from-compassion. One might almost think that they sensed that these consequences might prove disquieting. And disquieting they are. The ethic of devotion-from-compassion no longer has the character of a law, as we should wish it to have. It no longer embodies cut-and-dried commandments. It is fundamentally subjective, and leaves to each one of us an individual responsibility of deciding to what point our devotion should go.

Not only are there no longer any precise commandments: ethics has come to concern itself less and less with what is possible (the province, after all, of all law). It is constantly obliging us to attempt what is impossible, and to extend our devotion to the point at which our very existence is compromised. In the hideous times which we have lived through, there were many such situations; and many, too, were the people who sacrificed themselves for others. Even in everyday life, and although the ethic of devotion may not demand of us this last sacrifice, it often requires us to ignore our own interests and to relinquish our advantages in favour of others. Too often, alas! we manage to stifle our conscience, and with it our sense of responsibility. There are many conflicts, moreover, in which the ethic of devotion abandons us to ourselves. How often can a great industrialist congratulate himself on having given a post, not to the man who was best qualified, but to the man who most needed it? Woe betide such people if they decide, after one or two experiments of this sort, that the argument from compassion may always be overruled.

One last conclusion must be drawn from the principle of devotion: it no longer allows us to concern ourselves only with other human beings. We must behave in exactly the same way towards all living creatures, of whatever kind, whose fate may in some respect be our concern. They too are our kith and our kin, inasmuch as they too crave happiness, know the meaning of fear and suffering, and dread annihilation. To a man who has kept his feelings intact, it is quite natural to have pity for all living creatures. Philosophy likewise should decide to acknowledge that our behaviour towards them must be an integral part of the ethics which it teaches? The reason is quite simple. Philosophy is rightly apprehensive that this immense enlargement of the sphere of our responsibilities will deprive ethics of whatever chance it still has of framing its commandments in a reasonable and satisfying way.

The man who is concerned for the fate of all living creatures is faced with problems even more numerous and more harassing than those which confront the man whose devotion extends only to his fellow human beings. In our relations with animals and birds we are continually obliged to harm, if not actually to kill them. The peasant cannot rear all the new-born animals in his flock. He can only keep those which he can feed, and which will eventually repay what they have cost him. In many cases we have to sacrifice certain lives in order to save others. A man who rescues a strayed bird may have to kill insects or fish to keep it alive. Such actions are entirely arbitrary. What right has he to sacrifice a multitude of lives in order to save the life of a single bird? And if he kills off what he considers to be dangerous animals, in order to protect more peaceable ones—then there too he is in the realm of the arbitrary.

Each one of us, therefore, must judge whether it is really necessary for us to kill and to cause pain. We must resign ourselves to our guilt, because our guilt is forced upon us. We must seek forgiveness by letting slip no opportunity of being of use to a living creature.

How great an advance it would be if men could only remember the kindness that they owe to such creatures, and if they could refrain from harming them, through thoughtlessness! If we have any self-respect, where our civilisation is concerned, we must struggle against those feelings and those traditions—and they are many —which do violence to humanity. I cannot refrain in this connection from naming two practices which should no longer be tolerated in our civilisation: bull-fighting, where the bull is put to death, and stag-hunting.

Ethics is only complete when it exacts compassion towards every living thing.

There has been another great change in the position of ethics: it can no longer expect to be supported by a conception of the world which, in itself, justifies ethics.

In every age ethics has been supposed to conform to the true nature of the universal will which is made manifest in Creation. It was in conformity with this will that ethics issued its commands. Not only was religion based upon this conviction; the rationalist philosophies of the seventeenth and eighteenth centuries also took it as their base.

But the ethical conception of the world is based upon its own optimistic interpretation of that world. Ethics endows the universal will with qualities and intentions which give satisfaction to its own way of feeling and judging. But during the nineteenth century research—which after all can only be guided by regard for the truth—was compelled to admit that ethics can expect nothing and gain nothing from a true knowledge of the world. The progress of science consists in an ever-more-precise observation of the processes of nature. It is this which allows us to make use of the energies which manifest themselves in the universe. But at the same time these researches oblige us, in an ever greater degree, to relinquish all hope of understanding its intentions. The world offers us the disconcerting spectacle of the will-to-life in conflict with itself. One existence maintains itself at the expense of the other. In the world as it is we see horror mingled with magnificence, absurdity with logic, and suffering with joy.

How can the ethic of devotion be kept going without the support of a notion of the world which justifies it? It seems destined to founder in scepticism. This is not, however, the fate to which it is foredoomed. In its infancy, ethics had to appeal to a conception of the world which would satisfy it. Once it realises that devotion is its basic principle, it becomes fully aware of its nature —and, in doing so, becomes its own master. We too, by meditating on the world, and on ourselves, can come to understand the origins and the foundation of ethics. What we lack is complete and satisfactory knowledge of the world. We are reduced to the simple observation that everything in it is life, like itself, and that all life is mystery. True knowledge of the world consists in being penetrated by the mystery of existence, and of life. The discoveries of scientific research merely make this mystery yet more mysterious. The penetration of which I speak corresponds to what the mystics call "learned ignorance"—ignorance, that is to say, which at least grasped at what is essential.

The immediate datum of our consciousness, to which we revert whenever we want to understand ourselves and our situation in the world, is this: I am life which wants to live, and all around me is life that wants to live. Myself permeated by the will-to-life, I affirm my life: not simply that I want to go on living, but that I feel my life as a mystery and a standard of value. When I think about life, I feel obliged to respect all the will-to-life around me, and to feel in it a mysterious value that is the equal of my own. The fundamental idea of good, therefore, is that it consists in preserving life, in favouring it and wishing to raise it to its highest point; and evil consists in the destruction of life, in the injury of life, or in the frustration of its development.

The principle of this veneration of life corresponds to that of love, as it has been discovered by religion and philosophy in their search for the fundamental notion of good.

The term "reverence-for-life" is broader and, for that reason, less vital than that of love, but it bears within it the same energies. This essentially philosophical notion of good has also the advantage of being more complete than that of love. Love only includes our obligations towards other beings. It does not include our obligations towards ourselves. One cannot, for instance, deduce from it the necessity of telling the truth: yet this, together with compassion, is the prime characteristic of the ethical personality. Reverence for one's own life should compel one, whatever the circumstances may be, to avoid all dissimulation and, in general, to become *oneself* in the deepest and noblest sense.

Through reverence-for-life we enter into a spiritual relationship with the world. Philosophy has tried, and tried in vain, to build up some grandiose system that will bring us into contact with the absolute. The absolute is so abstract in character that we cannot communicate with it. It is not given to us to put ourselves at the service of the infinite and inscrutable creative will which is at the basis of all existence. We can understand neither its nature nor its intentions. But we can be in touch with that will, in a spiritual sense, by submitting ourselves to the mystery of life and devoting ourselves to all the living creatures whom we have the opportunity and the ability to serve. An ethic which enjoins us only to concern ourselves with human beings and human society cannot have this same significance. Only a universal ethic, which embraces every living creature, can put us in touch with the Universe and with the Will which is there manifest. In the world, the will-to-life is in conflict with itself. In us—by a mystery which we do not understand—it wishes to be at peace with itself. In the world it is manifest; in us, it is revealed. It is our spiritual destiny to be other than the world. By conforming to it, we live our existence, instead of merely submitting to it. Through reverence-for-life we come to worship God in a way that is simple, profound, and alive.